WHAT OTHERS ARE SAYING

I0053205

"*Leading from the InsideOUT* comes at a critical time. Now, more than ever, our political community and our business leaders need Kolb's wisdom to navigate today's uncharted seas. Through relatable stories, the reader discovers that the ability to lead from the inside and to build trust and community is within us all."

　　　　　　–Michael O'Brien, Peloton Coaching and author of
Shift: Creating Better Tomorrows

"This book is very much on point with what client organizations are looking for in anyone involved in leading. David provides a comprehensive roadmap that provides an excellent reference for both coaching professionals and developing leaders."

　　　　　　–Alex Grimshaw, CLO, SyNet Americas
Senior Partner, PPS International Limited

"*Leading from the InsideOUT* should be required reading for all leaders. Many modern leadership writers really don't know what it is like to lead—no matter how much research they do—so the success of many of these books depends largely on creating a convincing illusion. David's book is based on his successful leadership experience and therefore is based on reality and is written with great skill. It is an applied and thoughtful book."

　　　　　　–Mike Feinman, CEO, FazTex Restaurants, Inc.
Managing Partner, Central Texas Business Brokers

"*Leading from the InsideOUT* just may become an instant classic because it at once is both lofty in its reach and scope—the journey to authentic, enlightened leadership—while also down-to-earth in its humanity and conversational readability. Many times, Kolb writes as he likely coaches his executive clients, with inspirational candor and piercing depth so as to create a 'happening.'"

　　　　　　–Rick Brandon, PhD, Author of *Survival of the Savvy*,
Wall Street Journal Bestseller

"A must read book for a leader of any level who wants to expand their capacity to lead. *Leading from the InsideOUT* will force you to reflect deeply on your leadership style. David beautifully combines personal anecdotes with a range of references from ancient Homer's *The Odyssey* to Jim Collins' *Good to Great*."

　　　　　　–Lance Colwell, Vice President,
Biogen, U.S. Rare Disease Group

"Make no mistake, Kolb's Inside*OUT* is neither a recipe for the easy way nor a display of short cuts. It does, however, offer a principled and reliable map and compass that any leader, regardless of stage of development, will find invaluable."

–Malcolm Gauld
Executive Chairman, Hyde School

"This is not another 'leadership formula book.' You'll get to the heart of the matter, your *self*, which is a journey that's worth your investment!"

–Sharon Richardson, PhD, Medical Affairs Lead
Spark Therapeutics – U.S. Hematology

"David's model of leadership development is unique in the industry. This isn't a simple, task-oriented, self-help guide for leaders. It is a deep dive into the motivations, emotions, and personal attributes necessary to become someone that others will want to follow."

–Rev. Peter A. Friedrichs, Lead Minister
Unitarian Universalist Church of Delaware County

"In *Leading from the InsideOUT*, David has brought his wealth of life, leadership, and coaching insights into an impressive recipe for leadership discovery and development. If you, as I do, believe that leadership mastery can only be achieved by starting with an understanding of self and then by developing leadership capacities that are solidly rooted in this core, then you will find a treasure of insights by reading this book."

–Werner Eikenbusch,
Head of Talent Management, Americas, BMW

"Much work that is done to develop leaders is focused on leaders' outward actions—how they speak, how they plan, how they handle difficult and challenging situations. Of course these actions matter, but *Leading from the InsideOUT* brings our attention to the real work that makes the action possible and meaningful: an understanding of how to master ourselves in order to actually demonstrate deep authenticity."

–Kelly L. Fairbairn
President, PPS International Limited
CEO, SyNet Americas

LEADING FROM THE

INSIDE *OUT*

EXPANDING YOUR
CAPACITY TO LEAD

DAVID M. KOLB

Copyright © 2018 by David M. Kolb

All rights reserved
Printed in the United States of America

No part of this book may be reproduced or transmitted in any form or by any means, electronic or mechanical, including photocopying, recording or by any information storage and retrieval system, without the prior written permission of the author, except for the inclusion of brief quotations in critical articles or reviews and certain other non-commercial uses permitted by copyright law.

Inquiries to the author and requests for permission or information should be directed to the publisher at the email or postal address below.

Published by Prism
12 Estes Drive
Freeport, Maine 04032 USA
damoko@mac.com

FIRST EDITION

Kolb, David M.
Leading from the Inside*OUT*: Expanding Your Capacity to Lead

ISBN: 978-1-7322898-0-2

To Serena,

my partner

in life

love

laughter

and shared journeys

DISCLAIMERS

The author and publisher shall have neither liability nor responsibility to any person or entity with respect to any loss or damage caused, or alleged to have been caused, directly or indirectly, by the information contained in this book.

The purpose of this book is to inform and educate. The advice and strategies contained in this material may not be suitable to all leadership circumstances. For the best support, you should consult with a professional appropriate to your situation.

The author and the publisher have made every effort to ensure that the information in this book was correct at press time. The author and publisher do not assume, and hereby disclaim, any liability to any party for any loss, damage, or disruption caused by errors or omissions, whether such errors or omissions result from negligence, accident, or any other cause.

Names and identifying details in the stories of clients have been created to protect the privacy of actual individuals and to provide examples of various leadership characteristics.

It is not our job to remain whole.

We came to lose our leaves

Like the trees, and be born again,

Drawing up from the great roots.

–Robert Bly

CONTENTS

ABOUT THE AUTHOR

David M. Kolb is a teacher and coach. His focus is on enhancing interaction between people—especially for those in leadership.

His diverse professional path has shaped his unique approach. In his early career, he operated a residential construction company. He later earned his M.A. in clinical psychology from Antioch University, Los Angeles. He transitioned from his counseling practice to the corporate world where his articulate and passionate approach reached thousands of leaders seeking to increase their management skills. He was Director of Training for Ridge Associates, a principal consultant with PPS International Ltd., and currently is President of Prism, an executive coaching group.

Executives who are looking for excellence in the way they lead seek him out as coach and consultant. His clients span a range of industries including health care, technology, energy, and finance. He has also worked with educational and non-profit organizations. Even though he is most familiar with the people-side of the business, he helps clients balance their economic business necessities *with* the very real needs of the people actually performing the work.

From his years of work with leaders, he noticed that even when leaders use their best skills they still aren't guaranteed long-term effectiveness. In response, he developed the Inside*OUT* model so that new leaders as well as veterans would have a guide for developing the fundamental and sustainable capabilities for being a leader.

One executive said, "David swims with us in our water. He gets inside our business with us." This is because he is dedicated to helping his clients find ways to remove the complexity in their relationships so trust and truth can become their reputation.

He lives in Freeport, Maine, with his wife, Serena and their dog Demi. They love bicycle touring, paddling at their lakeside cottage, and sharing time with their families.

You may contact him at: damoko@mac.com

FOREWORD

There is no doubt that at this time in our evolution as a species we human beings need to also transform how we relate to the notion of leadership. Now, perhaps more than ever before, our global interdependence is an obvious reality. What happens in one part of the world is often inextricably linked to and thus influences what happens in another part. From a historical perspective, being so connected globally is relatively new, and it is creating a context that brings new lessons about what effective leadership means. While our growing interconnection enables many amazing opportunities for growth and enrichment, it also brings many risks and challenges that require us to think very differently about what we consider good leadership. Now, like never before, it really matters that we work on improving how we express leadership and how it manifests in our social, political, and financial institutions.

There is a growing need for us to ask ourselves new questions like: What sort of leadership is required to address the issues that extend beyond our own individual needs and experiences? What sort of leadership is needed when we think about ourselves as part of a whole system? Whether it involves tackling the desperate need for global organizations to address how we handle climate change and distribute natural resources, or how we create sustainable economic development that nurtures growth in trade and investment for all the world's people, or even how we think about humanity's actions extending beyond the physical boundaries of this planet as we continue to explore the wider universe, it is clear that a new relationship with leadership is required.

There is now compelling evidence that if we do not address the current social, political, and economic inequalities that we are facing in the world in a way which balances the needs and interests of all, our delay is going to have a detrimental impact on all of us. In today's emerging global community with challenges that extend beyond the localism and regionalism, it is simply outdated to sustain a sort of leadership that is about power, a focus on one's own interests or the interests of one's own group or clan first. This won't work anymore, and we need to find new ways.

Over half the world's population is now under the age of thirty, and 90% of those people live in developing countries. This fact alone means that we are forced to change our historical models of power, authority, and how we lead. It demonstrates the pace at which we will be required to readjust. In less than a generation, our world may be a very different place, and our current approach to leadership will most likely need to be very different as well.

As the pro-bono director of WYSE International, a global leadership development charity, for the last twenty-five years, I've had the inspiring and often very humbling experience of working with emerging leaders from over 115 countries who believe in a different form of leadership. WYSE International identifies and supports individuals who already possess vision and awareness and who are inspired to take up the challenge of leadership for the purpose of making a positive difference in their local communities and within the context of the global reality we now face. Through transcultural leadership development programmes followed by long-term coaching support, they develop new models of what cooperative leadership means in the global context, and then they apply what they've learned through transformative projects that have collectively impacted the lives of millions.

So, while the coming generations will inherit many seemingly intractable problems of enormous scale and complexity, my hope lies with the increasing number of young people who want to make a real difference and create a different form of leadership. With all the challenges that global citizenship brings, there also have never been more opportunities to connect, cooperate, educate, and share ideas.

There has never been a greater level of enthusiasm to interact and work together to create innovative solutions.

There is a strong and growing trend towards the importance of meaning and purpose in leadership. Many talented young people who typically become leaders and influencers want to do things that are meaningful. They want to contribute to something that is larger than themselves, create something that extends beyond their own personal gain. They want to feel like they are making a difference. And, of course, this is a need that is not just limited to emerging leaders. Professionally, since I work as a psychologist in the fields of leadership development and coaching, I have the privileged opportunity to support some incredibly talented and influential leaders in the corporate world. Many of them also crave a deeper sense of purpose in what they are doing.

I am pleased to say that the model presented in *Leading from the InsideOUT* is applicable to people on the journey of leadership development from any context. It provides the opportunity for individuals to create their own version of leadership based on what matters to them and what engages them in the challenge of bringing their vision of themselves into reality. The qualities and behaviours that are so clearly described in this book align closely with the journey of development that I have witnessed in many people from many walks of life.

Anyone interested in developing the capacity to lead needs to ponder, wrestle with, and come to a place of understanding about the three vital questions that *Leading from the InsideOUT* poses: Who am I? Why am I here? and Where am I going? These queries could be overlooked as being obvious or trite, but when placed in the context of taking up the mantle of leadership, they become profound. To have a meaningful sense of leadership identity, we must explore in detail who we think we are and why we think we are here. It cuts to the core of our beliefs about ourselves and our role in relation to others. To form a new identity, we confront new ideas, and we question that which we have held as important. Only then, can we identify somewhere or something meaningful to move towards. These are difficult questions that result in challenging conversations with oneself, questions that many people, even those who already hold positions of leadership, have never really taken the opportunity to investigate. Why? Because it's not easy. There are no easy answers, and it's potentially quite uncomfortable. However, if someone does invest time and energy in the task of understanding and developing a deeper sense of identity, they plant the seeds for a powerful sense of purpose to emerge, which can fuel and sustain future actions. Having leadership identity at the heart of the model demonstrates how important it is to continually work with these three questions, refining and developing our sense of identity as we grow and develop our capacity to truly become a leader.

The model for *Leading from the InsideOUT* describes seven capacities that serve as key factors for leadership development. From building a sense of leadership *Identity*, the reader is challenged to develop capacities for *Connection*, *Transparency*, *Innovation*, *Perception*, *Action* and *Replication*. In many texts on leadership development, the next step would be a series of tasks and guidelines for how you should do it. However, leadership doesn't work very well as a recipe, and the inner leadership described in this book requires more from us. *Leading from the InsideOUT* is a refreshing change from the usual set of instructions. Instead, it provides an overview of each capacity and brings each section of the model to life with stories and case studies that urge the reader to reflect, to cultivate self-awareness, and to understand the impact their behaviour has on those around them. The result is an invitation to develop each capacity and a provocation to continue to work on oneself to express leadership from one's deepest sense of self.

It's often said that the Indo–European origin of the word leadership is *leith,* which means "to cross the threshold" or "to go forth and die." While this does sound rather dramatic in today's context, there is no doubt that anyone who has tried to take up the challenge of leadership will recognize that truly leading does require one to make a real and significant change. It demands that we cross a threshold and see ourselves differently. It requires discipline to work on oneself and create alignment between our inner and outer worlds. It requires us to engage in the adventure of taking a journey without certainty of the destination and to be secure in ourselves and in the values that guide us. In a sense, this does demand us to metaphorically "go forth and die." We must take the older image or view of ourselves and work with it to birth a new identity, a new version from which we can engage differently with the challenges of leading.

In my experience of working with leaders both in the development context and in the corporate world, it seems clear that a different kind of leadership is starting to emerge, one that begins with leaders who take responsibility for leading themselves first and then take conscious actions towards meaningful ends that are inspired by their values and sense of purpose. I believe that everyone has potential for leadership, but many do not undertake the inner and outer work needed to develop the capacity to lead. This wonderful book provides a map to support people to begin and to pursue their leadership journey, to develop the knowledge, skills, and mind-set needed to take up the adventure of *Leading from the InsideOUT.*

–Dr. Andrew McDowell
Director, WYSE International
www.wyse-ngo.org
Senior Partner, TPC Leadership
April 2018, London, UK

INTRODUCTION

When we think about leadership, we immediately think about the people who are doing the leading. Leadership has faces. We recall the legendary ones who touched, moved, and inspired people to achieve only dreamed-of possibilities. Gandhi, Martin Luther King, and Mother Theresa are often among the first we remember. Depending on our interests, we have also been favorably influenced by other leaders representing science, technology, politics, and religion, regardless of our points of view within these disciplines.

Many of us have fallen into leadership roles because we were at the right place at the right time. We focused our interest or opportunity in a particular direction. And then, before we knew it, we became a team leader or a supervisor simply because we were in the job longer than anyone else or because it was the way we could get a raise in our pay. And some of us became really good at our jobs.

Today many individuals are being more deliberate and are preparing themselves to become tomorrow's leaders. These individuals are intentionally enrolling in programs for developing their leadership potential. From organizations whose missions are to expose young people to positive role models of leadership to business schools and universities with their more formal business curriculum, there are now many leadership development programs from which to choose.

Even though there exists a menu of options for how to become a skillful leader, each of us suffers from the misguided behavior of the infamous. It seems that each year brings another round of individuals in high places that choose to exploit their position and their followers. Organizations like Enron, Bernard L. Madoff Investment Securities, Volkswagen, Wells Fargo, The (Harvey) Weinstein Company, and Turing Pharmaceuticals represent just a few of the organizations that have suffered because of their leaders' ruinous decisions.

These failures of leadership affect employees, retirees, stockholders, and the public's trust in leaders in general. And certainly, business is not the only arena in which leaders violate the common trust. Remember Watergate? Clinton/Lewinsky? Catholic Priests? Penn State Football? 2016 Presidential elections? Rick Snyder, Governor of Michigan during the Flint water crisis?

And the list continues to grow by the day. These failures of leadership are generally not because men and women in high places don't know their business or their duties, though some had no business being in their roles in the first place. Rather, these failures of leadership tend to arise from an inner deficit, a gap in character and in consciousness. Such personal shortfalls often result in devastating commercial and social tremors. But these recent debacles are not the first times that leaders misused the confidence placed in them, nor are these examples the last time we can expect to see such major errors. As long as organizations have leaders, we can expect that some of the people in charge will fail in their leading.

What is a leader's responsibility? We believe that a person who wants to lead, or upon whom the role of leading is bestowed, must attend carefully to discovering and then expanding his or her *capacities* to lead.

Too often, society and organizations assign roles and responsibilities to individuals in high places without first making certain that this person has the capacity to execute the assignment. It's akin to filling a car with gas expecting that it will be operable without first checking to see that the engine, transmission, and tires are in working order, or more fundamentally that these vital elements even exist.

As a leader, your followers expect you to come to the job with whatever it takes to demonstrate that you possess the *capacities* required to lead. Organizations also share in this same responsibility when they place personnel in leadership positions.

Leaders are not only responsible for favorable fiscal and operational results but also accountable to an unspoken social contract that followers grant to those who lead.

Inside*OUT* provides a map for individuals to chart their course in becoming women and men worthy of the sacred trust that followers place in their leaders and for organizations to use as a model to ensure their leaders are ready for the job.

Inside*OUT* examines the fundamental ingredients that make up a leader. I began by looking at dozens of leadership models and approaches, asking the question: what guarantees that a given leadership skill or feature actually takes root and becomes natural? I began to wonder exactly what the components would be if leadership started from the inside and worked its way outward. If you're already a leader or if you're responsible for developing leaders for your organization, read on to discover the key factors and progressions that are critical to successful leadership.

The leaders described in this book are people who have deliberately cultivated their careers. As such, these individuals bring many life experiences to their leader role, yet when I met them, they were inadequate in some key leadership capacity. Even though they knew they lacked something, they still chose to do something about it. They chose to confront their situation and to grow by starting with themselves. They developed from the inside, out.

> *What lies behind us*
> *and what lies before us*
> *are tiny matters*
> *compared to what lies*
> *within us.*
>
> –Ralph Waldo Emerson

1

INSIDE *OUT* LEADERS

Leadership in a New Light

Imagine you're the captain of a sailing ship in the early nineteenth century. Your ship carries its cargo deep in its hold, well protected from the elements by solid wood decking. Your crew also lives below these decks. In fact, when crewmembers are not on duty, they are likely to be below decks eating, sleeping, or repairing gear and clothing.

The weather-resistant deck is intended to protect the cargo but in the same manner can be punishing for the crew. They live in nearly inhuman conditions—constant motion, cramped quarters, rancid food, and merciless gloom. As captain, your quarters are only slightly more habitable.

And then you hear about a simple invention that would make living on these stout sailing vessels more bearable for everyone—you hear about a specially cast piece of glass that is inserted into the solid decking: a deck prism.

This deck prism is an angular chunk of glass that is designed to multiply the quantity of sunlight that passes through it. This piece of glass is inserted into a small opening in the deck, and even though it is only a few inches in diameter, it both magnifies and redirects the sunlight into the more poorly lit areas of a ship.

You have suddenly made the interior of your ship much more habitable. Your crew will be healthier living in more natural light; they will likely be happier and more productive. And you will not need as many open flame lanterns. You have just increased your odds of delivering your cargo more safely and with a more able-bodied crew. And since shipping is your business, this small invention just lowered your costs and boosted your profits.

A shipwright must install these deck prisms in specific locations. The aim is to create the best illumination below decks while avoiding installation near any gear or particularly dirty locations on deck that might block or limit the sunlight. While some of these prisms were made from inferior glass, you seek out an excellent quality casting that is essential to creating a prism that allows the crew living below deck to benefit from its intended purpose.

Once you found the best prisms, simply installing a deck prism isn't sufficient to insure illuminated quarters. After you direct your purser to purchase quality prisms, you need to instruct your carpenter to install them where they can do their best work, and then assign crew to maintain and clean them for ongoing effectiveness. Remember, as captain, you're the one in charge of caring for your vessel.

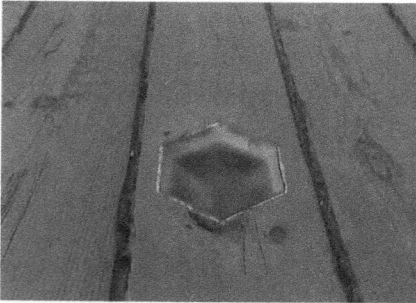

From a small opening in the ship's deck...

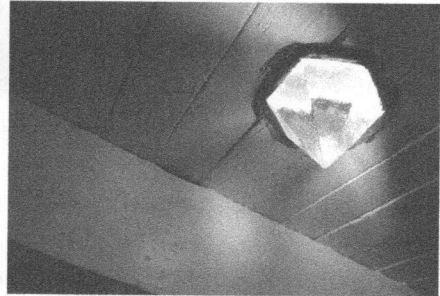

...a glass prism disperses sunlight below decks

The function of leadership is similar to that of the glass prism. Leaders must have the appropriate internal composition and characteristics in order to fulfill their duty. Then they must inhabit the place in an organization where they can be most effective. Moreover, leaders must constantly hone and maintain their skills to effectively guide their organizations and the people they lead.

This book focuses on the qualities that constitute a leader; in other words the development of a leader's components—their *capacity* to lead.

21st Century Leaders

Many leaders already possess effective leadership attributes. That's probably how they became a leader in the first place. But as we venture into the next century of highly complex global enterprises, our organizations will need leaders not only to be talented but to be consciously evolved as well. Such leaders will need to not only be highly skilled but also possess outstanding personal maturity. They will need to be enlightened.

Enlightened leading begins with leaders who accept that neither their title nor their position will guarantee that people will follow them. Though technical skills are necessary, they're not sufficient for becoming a leader. Leaders must also guide their personnel with a specific kind of humility. And this is an immensely difficult task given that they must fulfill their organization's objectives using the combined efforts of many other people.

Stakeholders expect leaders to know where they are going and to know how to navigate the uncertainties that will inevitably arise. These twenty-first century leaders need to be able to balance two forces at once: the expectations placed on them by their superiors or board of directors and the reality that they often don't know what to do because neither they nor their organization have ever before encountered the situation they face.

Ronald Heifetz, Founding Director of the Center for Public Leadership at the Harvard Kennedy School, describes leadership this way. "The adaptive demands of our societies require leadership that takes responsibility without waiting for revelation or request. One may lead perhaps with no more than a question in hand."[1]

For leaders to stand in this ambiguity, they must first be committed to rigorous self-examination. We have so often seen how a person who is thrust into a leadership position either becomes overwhelmed by its responsibilities and withdraws from the demands or assumes that along with the position comes the permission to act like a tyrant executive they saw on television.

How does a person begin the deep process of examining their leadership potential? It starts by looking inward and by developing one's capacities to lead before acting outwardly.

Capacity for Leading

In Inside*OUT*, *capacity* refers to one's potential or suitability to contain or to hold something. When we say that someone has leadership potential we are implying capacity. It's as if we can see something inside the future leader that they have not yet recognized in themselves.

What do we sense when we say that someone has potential? We're talking about the presence of forces that could evolve into actuality. You see, the word potential feels exciting, but it has no texture. It's enticing but lacks specifics. It's a tease to tell someone they have potential without giving them the keys to your insight.

In this book, I've attempted to describe those keys, those whiffs of future possibility, and the clues that led us to say that a person has leadership potential. When we look into that person's future, we are seeing their latent capacities to lead.

But, we cannot have leading without following. We cannot have capacities for leading without related capacities for following. When we aim to develop and expand our leadership capacities, we are engaging in an ancient, and unspoken, agreement, between those who will lead and those who will follow. This means that people who aspire to lead are entering into a web of complex relationships that requires self-awareness, respect of other, and organizational savvy.

In my executive development practice, the most challenging situations I've seen are those in which management has promoted a successful individual contributor without an introduction to, a modeling of, and a coaching process for the required leadership capabilities. I've worked with many people who were already good at their profession or trade before they became leaders but are now thrust into a complicated role without adequate preparation. Most organizations seem to assume that the natural career progression for a person who has mastered a task is to place them in charge of others. This promotion certainly addresses employees' expectations for periodic wage increases and career opportunities. Yet too many of those promoted are not prepared for their new supervisory job. In fact, it seems most organizations have little patience for insuring that these upwardly mobile employees are prepared for their new responsibilities.

As the authors of *The Leadership Pipeline* point out: "Perhaps the most difficult aspect of this transition is that first-time managers are responsible for getting work done through others rather than on their own."[2]

Here then is the first breakdown in leadership development. As a society, we place a greater value on acquiring degrees or experience in business, technology, or science than we do on preparing people for leadership. We expect people to spend years acquiring an education and considerable experience in order to become a professional in their area of expertise. Yet, as a culture, we do not expect the same from a leader. If we are to correct this deficit, we must all learn how to make effective leaders.

By definition, leaders are those who relate in some way with other people. *People* are the substance of a leader's work. No amount of education or experience in accounting or marketing, pharmacology or fluid dynamics will equip an individual for leading people. Leading is a social enterprise. So why don't we expect our leaders to be thoroughly schooled in the social sciences—psychology, sociology, anthropology, or other humanities—before they receive their leadership assignments? We have CEOs leading major organizations employing thousands of people and answering to huge numbers of stakeholders and yet their primary qualification is expertise in the technical or operational "product" of the organization. Many examples come to mind: the tech wunderkind who leads a multi-billion dollar enterprise, or the scientist who becomes CEO of a large biotech business, or even the engineer who is at the helm of a multinational industrial manufacturing company.

Even without this extended and specific preparation for leadership, we still somehow manage to have some individuals who do a pretty good job directing their organizations. They guide their employees in an identified direction and clearly have the ability to direct their staff who contribute graciously to the endeavor. Their staff stretch themselves to deliver on their leader's commitments while at the same time maintaining the high standards needed by those inside and outside the organization. These teams display a cooperative and collaborative spirit that not only results in the organization's success but in the joy and fulfillment of individual team members.

What makes the difference between the leaders who are doing a pretty good job and those many who struggle to adapt to a leadership role? It seems like some have magic while others don't.

What is this secret ingredient? What is this fundamental difference?

Leadership Capacities

Even though some of us strap various wings and other flight contraptions onto ourselves so we can fly through the air and feel nothing beneath our feet, we do not become birds. Likewise, assigning an employee to a leadership role, or even attaching leadership skills onto an employee, does not inherently make that person a leader. It's necessary for those who would become skillful leaders to first possess these seven capacities.

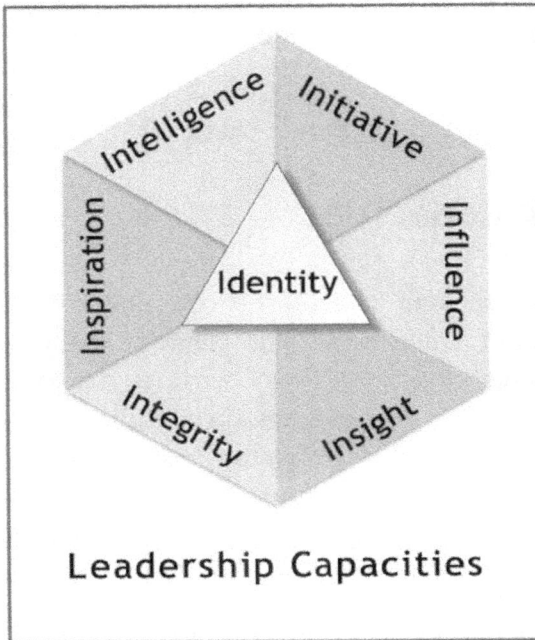

Leadership Capacities

Identity, the Capacity for Self-Mastery, equips the leader with self-management and self-direction and is at the core of a leader's constellation of capacities. Each of the other leadership capacities grows out of self-mastery.

Insight, the Capacity for Connection, links the leader to others.

Integrity, the Capacity for Transparency, supplies the leader with impeccable social currency.

Inspiration, the Capacity for Innovation, fuels the leader to be a source of creation.

Intelligence, the Capacity for Perception, engages the leader in multiple ways of knowing.

Initiative, the Capacity for Action, infuses the leader with sustained energy.

Influence, the Capacity for Replication, assures that the leader generates successors.

The content in each capacity begins like a seed and then expands in volume and in characteristics.

Expanding Capacities

The following map charts the course for becoming an Inside*OUT* leader. Each leadership capacity will be explained in the following chapters along with a drawing of that capacity. You'll use it to navigate through your development and to chart your progress. Notice how each capacity develops through five stages as it expands from the center outward. You'll begin your explorations at the center, with *Identity— Capacity for Self-Mastery*. Then you'll examine each of the other capacities in greater detail.

Individuals who seek to become leaders will undergo a transformation. Like the seed that a gardener plants in the soil, you will experience the first two stages of each capacity internally, entirely within your own consciousness and invisible to others. This process begins deep within your core and just like a germinating seed, the earliest work on a leadership capacity is a very private affair, but it's definitely not a passive process.

Once the seed sprouts, as you'll see in the third stage, growth occurs in direct response to the gardener's diligent efforts to provide a healthy environment for the plant by amending the soil, removing weeds, providing plenty of sunshine and water, and keeping the pests away from the tender sprouts. Similarly, a new leader must cultivate each stage of their leadership development.

As you move outward on the map, you'll come to stages four and five. And you'll discover that what began as an internal effort to comprehend and to shape each capacity gradually becomes external and affects other team members within your organization and eventually within the communities you and your organization touch. Each stage of development within a capacity encompasses and transcends the attributes and capabilities of the previous stages in that capacity. In this way, each capacity *develops exponentially.*

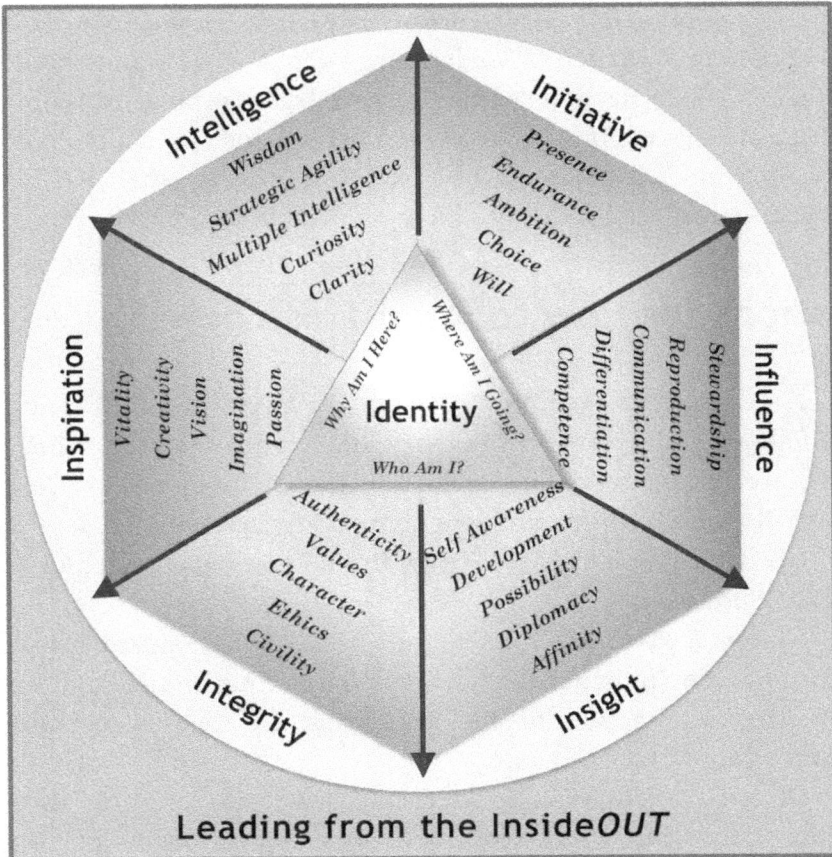

Leading from the Inside*OUT*

Additionally, as you deliberately attend to your personal and professional development within a specific capacity, every other capacity is simultaneously affected and evolves as well. In other words, as you're awakening, all the other capacities for leadership become aroused. Development of one capacity stimulates the development in each of the other capacities, creating a "rising tide lifts all boats" effect. This parallel benefit occurs because you are focusing your attention and effort on self-improvement and on being responsible in your interactions.

At first, this process of becoming a leader might sound self-centered. In a way, it is because we expect our leaders to possess a centered self. However, becoming a leader is not only a very personal experience, it is also a deliberate social phenomenon. Inside*OUT* leaders are people on fire, and their influence is felt on their teams, in their organizations, in their marketplace, and into their communities. Just as the ship's deck prism illuminated the crew's quarters, Inside*OUT* leaders ensure that followers have an illuminated path.

Options for How to Read This Book

Here are some options for how you might want to read the following chapters so you can quickly gain the most from the material in a way that works best for you given your style, your current situation, and your immediate inclinations.

Option 1: You're ready to dive in and you want to explore it all. Go for it.

Option 2: You don't have time to read the entire book right now. You're eager to check out the main premise and to view the architecture of the capacities. In that case, this chapter should be sufficient.

Option 3: You've allocated the time as long as the material fits you. We've identified some typical issues below to help you to determine which chapter might speak to your immediate concerns. In this way, you can triage your leadership challenges.

- ✓ **How can I maintain a steady course** instead of feeling pulled in different directions and often away from what I really want to do? I like change and new challenges, but my career feels scattered and not grounded to something fundamental.

  o *Start with Identity (page 15).*

✓ **I'm struggling with the people.** I like the position I have now, but I just don't get why some members of my team act the way they do. In fact, I'm irritated at some of them and would prefer they resigned.

  o *Read Insight (page 39), especially the later stages.*

✓ **I get feedback that I'm too abrupt and bossy.** Even though I'm the boss, I don't want to expose my organization to negative media or a summons from lawyers because I mess up. What should I do? I'm tired of tiptoeing around.

  o *After you read the chapter on Identity (page 15), check out Integrity (page 65).*

✓ **How can I fire up the team** and keep them excited about our work? Some days it's difficult to maintain my energy, and it seems like some team members keep running out of gas.

  o *Dive into the chapter on Inspiration (page 87), then go back to Identity (page 15), followed by Insight (page 39) and Influence (page 195).*

✓ **I'm beginning to feel like I'm burning out**. I'm good at what I do, but some days, I would just like to open up a small coffee shop and say good-bye to all the regulatory hassles and headaches in our industry.

  o *Start at Identity (page 15), but then go to the chapter on Intelligence (page 127) to explore other ways of navigating your interests.*

✓ **My time is never my own.** I don't know if I have a time-management problem or if I'm just in the wrong position. I feel pulled in a thousand directions. I'm constantly summoned by someone to do something or to go somewhere. How can I regain ownership of my days?

> o   *Begin with the chapter on Initiative (page 163). Then read Identity (page 15). After those two chapters just see what section appeals to you and dive in.*

✓ **How can I keep the good ones?** We're not getting as many young recruits coming into our industry as we did just five years ago. We are also not retaining managers who want to stay and grow their own skill sets. It seems like all they care about is the highest paying position wherever they can find it.

> o   *Start with chapter 8, Influence (page 195), then read Identity (page 15).*

Now it's time for you to dive in and prepare to stretch yourself. Many years ago, a wise person told me that my life would take on the shape and texture of the people I would meet and the books I would read. My wish for you is that this book will remain a companion with you on your journey and will form some of the texture of your future leading.

Yesterday I was clever
so I wanted to change
the world.
Today I am wise
so I am changing
myself.

–Rumi

2

IDENTITY
Capacity for Self-Mastery

Markus

He walked erect, looked me in the eyes, and as he thrust out his hand to greet me, his head tilted slightly to the right, and he introduced himself in a deep resonant voice. His thick dark hair and tall solid build seemed to announce that here was a very confident and obviously successful person. I was impressed. And it occurred to me that he used this well practiced behavior to do just that: impress.

Over the course of that first meeting, he talked about how he was already successful in his own business. He had measured success as double-digit growth in each of the past ten years, projects were completed on time, his customers were satisfied, the employees had steady work, and he had more-than-enough earnings to provide for him and his family.

Here was the poster-person of the successful American entrepreneur. What was missing? Where was the gap? Why did he seek coaching? Wasn't every business executive lusting after his life?

Gradually, and haltingly, as though he was inexperienced in the topic, he began to speak more personally. His marriage wasn't very strong, his teenage daughter and son were practicing their own versions of post-adolescent explorations, and he was very unhappy. Success, as he defined it, was the course he'd been on for the past fifteen years. And by at least one measure, he had reached his goal.

Yet there was this pesky notion that began to rise through his unhappiness: why?

"Why should I be so miserable when my business continues to grow?"

"Why have I spent all my life working to build a life for my now ungrateful wife and kids?"

"Why do I have to put up with all this *#@!> at my age?"

Over the course of several meetings with Markus, he asked more questions: questions that weren't seeking answers, at least from anyone outside himself. His voice echoed with an even deeper type of questing. He was revealing his restlessness and his core unhappiness.

For the next two years, Markus' life, as he had known it, unraveled. His wife left him, his children were much more interested in their friends than their miserable dad, and he sold his business. What he didn't know then was that the complete breakdown he felt he was having was actually the beginning of a breakthrough.

Then very slowly, he began to gain traction on the slippery downslope his life had become. He dug his fingers into the loose soil of possibility and planted seeds for a different future. He talked with other professionals who had faced dissatisfaction in their business-focused lives. He sought the guidance of a therapist so he could sort through the dusty corners of his forgotten self. And he wept. He grieved over the losses he created in his own life and the lives of those who meant the most to him.

Markus had arrived at the time in his life when he was ready to entertain the big questions—the ones he had deftly avoided during his business success. It took the dismantling of the life he knew before he was ready to look within for some meaning and purpose instead of quickly assigning blame outside himself—blame on the economy, his changing industry, his employees, or even his loved ones. He was beginning to comprehend a new picture of himself, and it didn't match the face-in-the-mirror he'd seen for so many years.

Markus had not only lost his leadership position in his business, he had also lost the respect of his family. Yet what was especially devastating to him was that he had lost, or had never defined, his own sense of who he really was. He was no longer master of his own life. He was without a sense of self.

When faced with so many painful losses, what was he to do? Where or to whom was he to turn?

Turning Inside*OUT*

Effective leaders must first know themselves so that their leadership is coherent and worthy of trust. Executives possessing this self-awareness are the ones who inspire others to follow and who insure that their organizations reach their strategic objectives. These leaders possess four traits; a clear sense of who they are, where they're going, the energy it takes to get there, and the ability to show others what's possible. However, before any of this can happen, those who want to truly lead must embark on a solitary inner journey. And like Markus, the journey often begins reluctantly and under severe conditions like the loss of a job, health, or loved one, or perhaps merely the threat of any of these occurring.

Some leaders only consider taking this inner journey after receiving crucial feedback, especially feedback that names behavior that these leaders can't see in themselves.

Leaders who are transformed through their own ordeal tend to be more qualified to lead. They have developed the courage and humility needed to become aware and sensitive to other's expectations of them and the weight of their leadership position.

Everyone's life is full of challenges, but leaders who have first consciously navigated their own human terrain are those who ultimately earn the most trust. Their followers perceive that this is someone who has their back—both emotionally and physically—and will act-in-kind to help them reach the organization's goals.

Each of us know of individuals in leadership roles who knew their place in the organization's endeavor, but who failed at leading because they had not effectively developed a firm nucleus of self awareness and character.

Such individuals are not followed because they cannot generate and sustain the energy that's required to persevere in the fulfillment of their own potential, let alone in the realization of their organization's vision. They are either too immature in their journey, or they have deliberately discarded the counsel of wiser and more experienced leaders. Subsequently, how can you insure that you'll become a trusted leader?

Most people move into a leadership role because of some indication that they would probably function well in this new role. Their style of interaction has already been formed out of their innate makeup, life experiences, and through the patterns they developed over many years in human relationships.

The leaders I've worked with already had possessed some assets that supported their role before I met them. Many of them had earned their place in their organization. A few were encouraged by their supervisor or human resources representative to seek coaching. Yet each leader also had some hint or some yearning that they could be even more effective, that they had not quite found the magic potion, that there was still something missing from their very core.

Identity—Capacity for Self-Mastery

For millennia, at the shrine of Apollo in Delphi, the inscription "Know Thyself" has beckoned seekers to take a solitary inner journey. This engraved injunction reminds us that we have a common human longing to make sense of our own existence. The leaders who deliberately see their inner enterprise as the first place to "do business" will be rewarded with insights that become guidance, first for themselves and then for their organizations.

To know oneself requires answers to the same three key questions that Markus needed to be asking:

Who am I?
Why am I here?
Where am I going?

Answers to these questions rarely appear suddenly. Instead, as in most heroic ordeals, the answers tend to reveal themselves gradually and only to the persistent seeker.

Just how does one deliberately embark on this journey of forging a durable and trustworthy sense of self? Of the discovery and ownership of one's *Identity*?

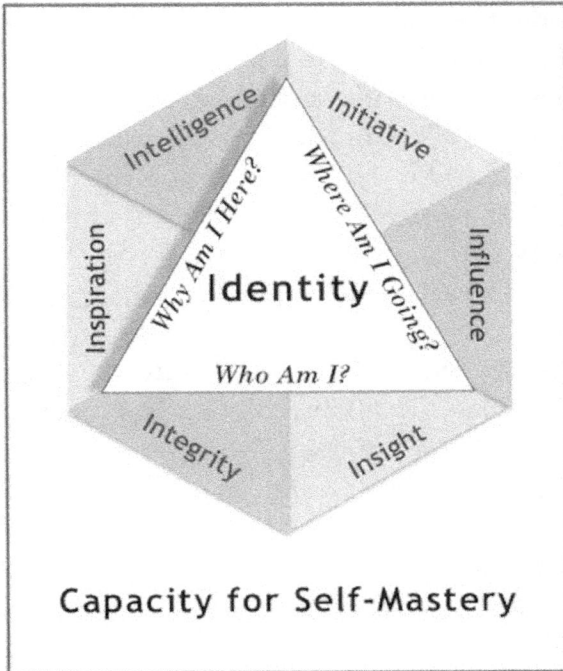

Capacity for Self-Mastery

Who Am I?

How might you answer this very personal question that can arise from within the silence of your mind? Or suppose a friend was to ask you, how might you answer?

Don't worry. It's unlikely that anyone will ask since in our society people don't ask the "Who are you?" question, but instead they ask, "What do you do?" After all, this question is more acceptable in a society that seems to value accomplishments over personhood.

If someone were to ask who you are, how would you respond? Would you describe your position in the organization, your role? Would you talk about your title or your job? Or would you describe your qualities or perhaps your values? Or would you scramble to regain your footing by describing what you are *not*?

In the responses that I've heard to this question, people frequently identify themselves by their career, "I'm an engineer by training, but currently I'm the VP of Operations." Or their roles, "I'm a wife, mother, sister, or daughter." Or their temperament, "I'm quick to make a decision." Or even with a dismissive, "I'm in Sales." People use their various ways of seeing themselves to give others a glimpse into who they think they are.

Whenever we say, "I am ___*(fill in the blank)*___," we reveal only a small portion of ourselves. Depending on the situation, you might identify with your physical state, e.g. "I'm tired," or with your emotions, e.g. "I'm really excited about that," Or with your thoughts or opinion, e.g. "I think the team must raise its standards." These comments are clues to how you see yourself—at least in that moment. Just listen for what follows "I am..." when you speak.

In still other conversations, you might hear yourself say something like, "A part of me wants to _____, but another part of me thinks _____." Though this comment might reveal ambivalence about the topic, it's more likely that you're giving credence to the reality that you're composed of more than one part. In fact, we all are comprised of many parts.

In the early part of the 20th century, Italian psychiatrist, Roberto Assagioli, conceived a practical understanding of the psyche. His work became known as Psychosynthesis, and he contributed to our understanding of how we function and how to develop self-mastery. In Psychosynthesis, he spoke of our parts as subpersonalities.

You might recall a time when you were in a mental tug-of-war because you needed to make a decision. For example, in the above paragraph, we hear that inner dialogue out loud as, "A part of me wants to _____, but another part of me thinks _____." Reread the previous sentence and actually add your own relevant content to the sentence. Go ahead...

When you heard yourself say the sentence, you most likely experienced an inner polarity. Each pole was pulling on something that you value but from a different direction. This is one small example of just two of your many parts.

In her book, *Multiple Mind*, clinical psychologist Gretchen Sliker describes another way to recognize our parts.

> The many roles we play in the world are subpersonalities. In one setting my behavior is that of a polished, dignified, and capable professional; in another setting I am the kind, gentle, and joyful parent celebrating the delight of my children. My body posture and movement, my voice and vocabulary are different as I play each role. Yet these roles are not external to me, they are who I am." She goes on, "The Renaissance man, by definition, is a person of multiple subpersonalities. Such a person might be, for instance, a scientist, a playwright, a musician, and a lover...[1]

Each of us is the expression of the various different textures in our psyche. We actually do pretty well managing our parts so they don't hassle each other too much. Yet occasionally, we stumble, and we trip over ourselves. We become so identified with one of our parts that we act in ways that in hindsight seem incredible, maybe even embarrassing, to our other parts.

Take Markus, as an example. A part of him was the picture of business success in his starched white button-down oxford shirts, while another part was failing in his most important relationships. He could lead others in his business, but he wasn't able to lead in his own family.

Exactly how did Markus arrive at this predicament? Subpersonalities develop in response to our many needs as a young child. In fact, by around two years of age, a child might already display the early presence of subpersonalities in their many and varied forms. As the child ages, his life experiences form even more patterns of behavior, roles, and ideas. Subpersonalities become even more richly textured and solidified, and by adulthood, this child will function quite skillfully because of the many years of practice his parts had at getting their needs met.

For example: You might be quick with a comment—words that direct others toward your input. When faced with an opening in conversation, or perhaps you don't even wait for an opening, you decide that a good defense is a good offense. You assert quickly and powerfully. This part of you dominates others without even being aware of its impact.

Or alternatively, you might be slow to show a reaction when others assert themselves. You might pause, or perhaps even freeze, before commenting or committing to an idea or action. In your head, you might even be ridiculing yourself for not engaging more quickly, and as a result, you may have already accepted some derogatory labels to describe yourself; labels like "weak" or "slow." Or you might have another part that quickly steps in and rationalizes for this slow-to-react part by actually referring to it as cautious, careful, or even thoughtful. "There's a part of me that is ready to buy the car now, but another part that first wants to check *Consumer Reports*."

You can see by these examples how our entire *Identity* is filled with many parts that form a dynamic dance of many pairs of opposites. Most of the time, this kind of candid conversation isn't verbalized. In fact, we're not even aware of the tension in our psyche until some external stimuli triggers us, and we *impulsively* act or speak from one of our "offended" parts.

Each of us is like the Renaissance man—composed of many different interests, behaviors, ideas, and emotions. We have a complexity of parts. So how is this inner tug-of-war handled? Do you succumb to being a bland mixture of indistinct averages? Or is there a dominant force, a bossy parent part that overrides the input of your other parts? Or perhaps you have a tiebreaker in your head, a benevolent referee. How is your inner crowd managed? How do any of us succeed in our human interactions since each of us is like a bubbling cauldron of potential chaos? Though we have our parts, who is the one that directs these many parts? Where is the "I?" I'll answer the question in this way.

The Orchestra

Imagine that I have two tickets to the concert tonight at Symphony Hall, and I ask you to join me. We arrive in our seats about twenty minutes before the scheduled starting time. As we chat about our journey to this magnificent facility, we notice the activity on the stage. Musicians are arriving; some are coming in quite casually, while others have been at their seats for several minutes already. Some are unpacking their instruments; others are already tuning theirs. The sounds are familiar yet discordant. Some of the musicians are chatting with their colleagues, and others are practicing some of their upcoming passages. They are each getting ready to play their own part.

You look at your watch and see it is nearly starting time. Suddenly the musicians become still, the audience quiets, and from the corner of the stage, the maestro walks to the podium, raises the baton, and the music begins.

We watch, and we listen as the various parts of the orchestra act as one. The crisp purity of the sound, the tempo, and the harmony created by the musicians give us great joy and an evening filled with listening pleasure.

The difference between the cacophonies we heard before the concert started and the harmonious symphony that washed over us not only happened because it was "show time" but also because there was an organizing center—the presence and function of the maestro.

Our own inner landscape is similar to the orchestra. We too have many functional parts. Each part might prefer its own favorite piece of music by its own favorite composer. Or a part might prefer passages that show off its unique characteristics and specialness. However, without the guidance of our inner maestro, others trying to work and live with us could rightfully accuse us of being competitive, harsh, self-centered, or even aloof. Perhaps you've already heard comments like these from others.

Our Inner Maestro

Ideally, each of us operates like an orchestra—a well-played performance by our many parts guided by our inner leader. Like the maestro, our inner leader does not make any music at all but instead directs the contributions of our many internal parts. The process can get tricky since most of the time we're operating *unconsciously* out of our subpersonalities, and we forget that we possess an inner leader. Without realizing it, our sense of who we are aligns with whatever part we're playing. This very act of identification is incredibly fluid, and that is why we can so easily say, "A part of me wants ____, and another part wants ____." In this case, our *Identity* is swinging between at least two parts, and we feel conflicted.

However, the moment we notice ourselves doing this, something else has entered the equation, an "observer." If we can notice our parts, then we cannot simultaneously be those parts. Who is the observer? Is it another *part*? Perhaps it's a part that does more than merely notices. Maybe it also evaluates or critiques what is observed.

This judging function sounds like another part, not an impartial observer. Many people have developed a powerful inner critic who is always ready to step in and take on roles that were probably first introduced to us by a parent, teacher, or coach; someone who may have been living out of their own inner critic and were thus unable to see a bigger possibility for you, the growing child in their care.

Remember the orchestra? The maestro did not use an instrument but only observed and directed the parts to make the appropriate music with *their* instruments. When your inner leader is functioning like the maestro, it's directing the contribution of your various parts. When you're identified with your maestro, you're in the place of "I," not in a role identified as a part. Here is when you truly and declaratively can simply say, "I am."

Psychologists refer to the "I" as the "self." The "I" is like a high-functioning executive in an organization—one who notices the needs, chooses the appropriate de*part*ment that will respond, directs others to fulfill those needs, and monitors the satisfactory completion of the effort. The "I" brings consciousness to the system. It brings a self-observing feedback loop that results in conscious action. When we're identified with our inner leader, our maestro, we experience what the philosopher poet Fernando Pessoa wrote, "My soul is a hidden orchestra; I know not what instruments, what fiddle strings and harps, drums and tamboura I sound and clash inside myself. All I hear is the symphony."[2] We are simply the one at the center of our inner organization, directing the functions, feelings, and opinions of all our parts. I *am* the self, and I *have* many different parts.

As you explore and grow into an understanding of who you are, you might occasionally hear an inner voice say, "So what?" This questioning is how we humans make sense of everything. As soon as we comprehend "what" something is, we immediately want to know "why" it is. Listen to a three-year-old child. Their incessant "why" is their way of comprehending their experiences through wonder and language.

The three questions that comprise *Identity*—who am I?, why am I here?, and where am I going?— don't need to be answered sequentially though one might choose to explore them in that order. Rather, each question seems to depend on the answers to the other two. In this way, the leader who diligently seeks to know the self will loop repeatedly among the answers to all three questions in a continual and evolving manner throughout life. Now, let's look at the next question.

Why Am I Here?

In the course of an executive coaching relationship, I asked my client, "So why are you here?" We both understood that I wasn't referring to that moment, in that room, but rather to the cosmic *here*. I'm not sure which startled her more: my question or her own response.

"I don't know...*(long pause)*...I haven't really thought about it that much...*(an even longer pause)*...how could I ever figure it out? How could I ever know why I'm here?"

Having asked herself the question, she could no longer plod through her life by going to meetings and writing reports, ignoring that there just might be a reason she was alive. She could not face her probable, almost certain, future unless she awakened to the answer. In a short time, she seemed genuinely ready to examine possible answers, and at our next meeting, she said that she had already begun to read two books on the subject. She had started on a mission to uncover an answer to why she was alive.

As Markus dove into the turbulent sea-of-his-own-making, he also began to wonder about his purpose. Like so many of us, he had been living a life that had his own interests firmly on center stage. Even though he was providing for his family, he knew that was not really why he was on this planet. Caring for our families is our baseline responsibility; he was doing that. Yet his attention to his family flowed more from his own self-interest rather than from an attitude of deep commitment and love. Instead, his opinion of his own magnificence was upheld by having a pretty wife and accomplished children surrounding him.

Now he faced the big question. Why was he here? Why was he still breathing?

Purpose

Unfortunately for many of us, the question of purpose doesn't get faced until the possibility of death scares us into self-examination. This can happen when we are actually looking at mortality, but it can also occur with the death of a dream or a relationship. "Oh why?" is the desperate cry of many when our well-planned life goes off the rails and we face loss. This is when we seem to be most open to exploring a purpose-driven life. And this is why some individuals use these existential moments to reacquaint themselves with matters of faith, spirit, and the Divine.

Richard Warren, in the book *The Purpose Driven Life*, writes, "Everyone's life is driven by something. What's the driving force in your life? Right now a problem, a pressure, or a deadline might be driving you. Or you may be driven by a painful memory, a haunting fear, or an unconscious belief. There are hundreds of circumstances, values, and emotions that can drive your life."[3]

We're surrounded by the question, "why." Think back to a time when you approached your supervisor with a proposal. Remember how you faced a barrage of questions that challenged what you thought was your well-thought-out-plan? Your boss was acting like any practical-minded executive would—frequently wondering *why* a proposal from an employee would be more profitable, or more efficient, or more customer-focused than the status quo. And you knew from your own experience, and from what your colleagues reported about their previous trips to the corner office, that you must be prepared with answers so you could face the challenge.

As adults, and bosses, we're similar to children in this way. We need to make sense of new input. This is a natural part of being human, of being conscious. In fact, it seems as though it is vital to becoming even more aware, more conscious. Consequently, we ask why.

Many executives seem quite eager to ask the "why" question when it's externalized—when it's directed at someone else. However, many aren't as comfortable looking inside themselves for answers to why. They don't want to go there. I wonder what they fear. Perhaps they're afraid to relate to the painful stuff? Perhaps they don't want to slow down the pace they're on. No, to do that would interfere with their drive.

How about you? You're riding high, or at least sitting upright. You feel pretty good, your endorphins are kicked in, and like a caffeinated wunderkind, you just don't see the value in negativity. In fact, you're not aware that anything needs correcting in your center. Hey, if it's not broken, you don't need to fix it, right?

If this describes you then clearly you're identified with a belief that is driving your life, and you would do well to figure out which of your *parts* is identified by that belief. However, the measure of a well-found leader is neither a euphorically absence of pain, nor a persistent misery that is fueled by some sort of worry. The measure of a mature leader is the presence of self-mastery. Unless you can clearly articulate an answer to the first question, who am I?, then it's important for you to go back to the beginning of this chapter and reestablish your *Identity*—who you think you are.

Though all this work around *Identity* might seem to you to be a form of navel gazing and self-absorption, the process is only self-centered if the process doesn't yield the opening to that-which-is-larger than oneself. Wrestling with why we are here brings us into relationship with something outside of our self. For many people, this means service to a cause that is greater than their own.

I have read many stories about people who have had this kind of awakening. One story was of mountaineer Sir Edmund Hillary when he was on track to his ultimate achievement, to be the first to summit Mount Everest. While on the trek to base camp, he saw the living conditions of many of the Nepalese people. Upon his successful climb and the subsequent fame, he returned to Nepal to respond. He was especially affected by the lack of education for the children, so he leveraged his resources to establish schools for these children and to build hospitals for the villagers. When reaching for ultimate experiences, many adventurers and explorers face awesome conditions that arouse a relationship with something greater than themselves and permanently shift their approach to life. In this instance, Hillary's personal achievements certainly resulted in his purposeful generosity.

The question, *Why am I here*, urges us out of our personal interests and, like Hillary, calls us to larger more generous efforts. The mere process of answering the question implies there is a call, something to which we respond. "I'm convinced that most of the time, *that's* what the voice inside of us is telling us to do. *To live for more than ourselves*," says Wes Moore. "It's the truth that hunts us down, our common calling. And when we answer that call, we'll find that the world's challenges and our own work inevitably meet."[4]

So why are you here? What is the meaning to your life? What is your purpose? What is your unique contribution to the world? Executives who are simply good at something are not necessarily leaders. Highly paid technicians with titles don't necessarily inspire others to follow. Discovering why you're still breathing—why you're still here on this planet— will result in direction, ambition, and confidence both for yourself and for those around you. Do you know your purpose?

Knowing your purpose prepares you then for where and how to express that purpose.

Where Am I Going?

"If you know the why, you can live any how."
–Friedrich Nietzsche

Once you know *why*, then your journey into the question, *where am I going*, becomes the direction you give to your life's purpose. It determines how your purpose is applied in your daily life. Look at your calendar for the past several months. Does it specifically reflect a person living out their purpose? Can you see your purpose showing through the reminders, meetings, and appointments on your calendar?

Nietzsche implies that the antidote to the aimlessness that some leaders seem to have is in their innermost self. He reminds us that our ability to persevere is linked to a cause that is real for us. It's like being plugged into a custom-designed source of energy. Yet, those who first seek their "what" or their "how" without having first discovered their "why" can spend a lot of energy merely trying to get traction. Their efforts can feel to them like force-fitting themselves into someone else's shoes.

Where are you going? What is your trajectory? What is the direction of your life? Is there a focus? What work have you undertaken? Your answers to these questions embody your cause, and your cause is where and how you apply your calling or purpose. When leaders know who they are and can articulate their purpose, they can become influential in their world for all the right reasons. The individuals I've met who are living out their purpose don't talk about stress. Though they're energized, busy, and move with drive, they do not appear worried, stressed, or frantic. They are clearly on a mission. And they're always immensely productive.

Asking why you're here does not necessarily oblige you to abandon your current career or occupation. Sometimes, the shift that occurs from asking the big questions leads people to discovering that what they're *doing* now is connected to their purpose. Some people find they can retool their current work while others will be drawn toward new work that truly fulfills them. Seekers cannot continue in activities that merely support their standard of living.

As an awakening leader, you might have already found purposeful fulfillment in your work. But what about your employees, what about others in your organization for whom you have responsibility? Are you helping them to experience an equal measure of personal fulfillment in their work?

We live in a wildly shifting work culture, and leaders must act to shape the workplace environment and the opportunities for workers. And as a leader, you have responsibility to make certain that your employees can find meaning in their work too.

In his book, *The Work*, entrepreneur, activist, and Army officer Wes Moore quoted anthropologist and activist David Graeber who described the contemporary state of work this way. "Huge swathes of people, in Europe and North America in particular, spend their entire working lives performing tasks they secretly believe do not really need to be performed. The moral and spiritual damage that comes from this situation is profound. It is a scar across our collective soul.... How can one even begin to speak of dignity in labour when one secretly feels one's job should not exist?"[5]

The difference in those organizations that are filled with people living on purpose and those that are simply attempting to return a profit to their stakeholders seems to be the presence of individuals who already know what they will do with their one precious life.

Your Cause

Every organization I've ever worked with has had some kind of mission statement. When I would ask about it, no one could tell me exactly what it was; consequently, I would explore their website. Occasionally, it was engraved on the reception area walls. Yet, I often wondered why it wasn't on the tips of the employees' tongues. Why was the mission relegated to a remote position behind conversations about budget, or market share, or downsizing?

Organizations are just like their constituents. Deep reflection on purpose, mission, or direction is often ignored until moments of pain and loss. There is nothing like a series of unprofitable quarters, serious product recalls, or furious investors to force an organization to reexamine its direction.

The same is true for individuals. Many leaders I've worked with do not (or cannot) articulate their personal mission let alone link their day-to-day work with their purpose. In fact, most of the people I've talked to about their life's work don't even seem to realize the level of satisfaction and purposefulness that could be available to them.

In their book, *Work Reimagined*, Richard J. Leider and David A. Shapiro wrote.

> People tend to see their work in one of three ways, and the satisfaction they derive from that work correlates closely. The distinctions are these: People who have jobs are mainly focused on gaining material benefits from work...The work is not an end in itself, but instead is a means that allows individuals to acquire resources needed to enjoy their time away from the job.

> In contrast, people who see what they do as a career have a deeper personal investment in their work and mark their achievements not only through monetary gain, but through advancement within their field. This advancement often brings higher status, increased power, and higher self-esteem.

> Finally, people with callings find that their work is inseparable from their lives. A person with a calling works not only for financial gain or career advancement,

but also for the fulfillment that doing the work brings to them.[6]

One of my clients, Geoff, had this epiphany when he realized that at his core his true purpose was to support and coach his staff. He shifted his work from his ego-stroking, global, jet-setting business expansion to intimate conversations with each member of his team. Instead of convening sales meetings in exotic places like Dubai, he focused on team and individual learning retreats.

It so happened that his team was located on nearly every continent so he still traveled a lot, but his actions were now aligned with the *who* he really was, and with *why* he was here. Rather than promoting his own visibility, he now focused on his team members—assisting each of them to become successful agents in their own lives and work. And you can probably imagine the multiplied impact his thirty-five awakening and supported team-members are having in their regions around the world.

Geoff didn't change his career. He didn't even need to change his business card. He changed himself. He became a maestro, and his cause was fueled by his purpose. He is now a different person, and the people that he said he cared about are now actually experiencing his caring guidance. Plus his global organization is positively impacting other leaders and organizations around the world. Yet not all journeys of personal discovery are as seamless as Geoff's transformation.

Your Quest

Many indigenous societies around the world develop their young people by putting them through an arduous coming of age event. These experiences have many forms and rituals, but what they have in common are rites-of-passage activities that cause the initiate to seek answers to the *Identity* questions–*who am I, why am I here*, and *where am I going*.

Often referred to as a vision quest, these times of solitude are designed so that young people can find their totem—it might be an animal that becomes a life-long teacher or a unique connection with the spirit of an ancestor or another source of power or influence in the community. The initiate would often experience some form of guidance or protection from their totem during the ordeal. This would become a uniquely individual connection that is forged and maintained by cultural beliefs. The transformative effect of a vision quest is similar to the experience that Leider and Shapiro describe in their book. "The word 'calling' was used originally in a religious context where people were understood to be 'called' by God to do morally and socially significant work."[7]

Since the 1980s, there have been many opportunities in the U.S. and Europe for adults to participate in weekend retreats that offer a vision-quest type of experience. In the popular youth program Outward Bound, there is a segment when participants spend time alone foraging for food and water and erecting their own shelter in order to create the circumstances through which the "initiate" might discover a previously untapped source of guidance and strength. All of these quests create conditions that propel the participants to form experiences and beliefs for who they think they are and to find their place in the world.

In 1986, during a time of struggle and seeking, I had several vision questing experiences, including one very long "sweat lodge" during which I traded huge amounts of perspiration for some wise guidance and insight that shaped my career and remains with me even today.

Your own answer to *where am I going* might come to you in a single event, or it might arrive slowly over the course of days, months, or even years. Nevertheless, it seems certain that the answer will not come unless you diligently quest.

Coda

Remember Markus? He lost his business, his marriage, and for a time, his life was dangling on the slimmest of threads. And then he gradually climbed out of despair. He discovered that his life had purpose and he walked forward by remaking himself. He achieved a graduate level degree and received, as he described it, a *third degree* from the school of life.

He found his voice and eventually became an instructor with an organization that conducted management seminars for business leaders. When I last saw Markus, he was focused on his new career and had mended his relationships with his children. He added that it took a while longer for him to find a life partner who would really believe in him.

He recently wrote to thank me for my influence in his life and to say that he had joined a consulting firm in Seattle. He was very happy and focused about the direction he was giving to his life. It looks like his inner maestro is directing his orchestra.

Who are you then? When you examine your *Identity*, you will see what comprises your energetic center. As an emerging leader, you are now ready to explore how this experience of your centered self shows up in your life and in your work. You will be able to identify and articulate this approach to knowing yourself. Your effort is not so much a process of acquiring an ever-increasing set of tools or skills, as it is an expansion of your *Capacity for Self Mastery*.

Fred Kofman and Peter Senge, from MIT's Sloan School of Management, describe the experience of *Identity* this way.

Newtonian physicists were startled to discover that the core of the atom, at the center of matter there is...nothing, no thing, pure energy. When they reached into the most fundamental building block of nature, they found a pregnant void—stable patterns of probability striving to connect with other patterns of probability. This discovery revolutionized the physical sciences, initiating the quantum era.

By the same token, we are startled to discover that at the core of the person, at the center of selfhood there is...nothing, pure energy. When we reach into the most fundamental basis of our being we find a pregnant void, a web of relationships. When someone asks us to talk about ourselves, we talk about family, work, academic background, sports affiliations, etc. In all this talk, where is our "self"? The answer is nowhere, because the self is not a thing.[8]

The self is simply energy that directs the functions of your being. Now let's examine the other six capacities for leading that, like *Identity,* are first experienced within your core and then are naturally and irresistibly expressed outwardly to your organization and ultimately to the world at large.

When we know ourselves
to be connected to all others,
acting compassionately
is simply
the natural thing to do.

–Rachel Naomi Remen

3

INSIGHT
Capacity for Connection

Elizabeth

It had been a tiring day of balancing the differing needs of some very vocal participants in a team-building session that I was facilitating. Back in my hotel room, I finally had time to read my over-flowing email inbox.

One message stood out from the rest. Subject..."Help"

It was from a vice-president in one of my client organizations. I had never met Elizabeth, but she was reaching out because she had heard about me from a client of mine within the company. I replied with an appointment time for a phone call.

When we connected, she told me about feedback she had recently received from her manager and several of her peers. Their message was direct, and it shocked her enough to reach out for "Help."

"Here's what they said," she told me. "They said that I was intimidating and that I often belittle my direct reports. They said that my people avoid me when they have key info about my department. They said that my direct reports are going to other senior managers behind my back. Plus they accused me of wasting their time in senior team meetings because they need to manage my emotional outbursts. They said that they value my point of view, but for some reason, they don't like how I deliver it. I'm just trying to get their attention."

She took a breath and then said, "They seemed to give me an ultimatum. They said I had to change me, not everyone else around me. What can I do to change their minds about me?"

Clearly, the feedback had grabbed her attention. Her "Help" email to me came within twenty-four hours of receiving the feedback. She said that normally she would have become defensive, but she was ready to try a different approach.

I asked her to talk to me some more about what they had said. She quickly replied that her boss, peers, and some of her staff just didn't understand her...they didn't get how committed she really was. She seemed genuinely perplexed that her own intentions were so misunderstood. Later in our conversation, I asked how she would most like her future to be, and she described a clear image of a strong, caring leader. So I agreed to begin a coaching relationship.

To start the process, we created a customized assessment that began when I interviewed her key stakeholders. To measure her perception of her behavior and compare it with that of others, we designed a series of questions based on her own intentions for improvement, on the comments from her supervisor and peers, and on comments from her staff.

At first Elizabeth's predicament looked like a typical "self-awareness" dilemma. However, what I eventually discovered was an important gap that I frequently find when working with executives. Elizabeth was a driven executive split off from the source of her own passion. When she was dealing with others, it was easy for them to interpret her fervor as anger, judgment, or lack of caring about them.

Elizabeth was surprised by the results of the assessment. Each rater, as well as Elizabeth herself, gave a score for each item. In addition, some raters provided anonymous comments and examples that helped Elizabeth to understand how others experienced her.

I handed her the envelope and she began reading the results. I invited her to simply use her highlighter to mark any item to which she had an immediate reaction. I encouraged her not to stop and analyze a comment or rating but to push on and read the next item until she had completed the entire report.

As she read through the report, she fell uncharacteristically silent. I watched her facial expressions and her body language, carefully looking for how and when the impact of the scores reached her. I could see that she was beginning to struggle. Her eyes narrowed slightly. The edges of her mouth became firm and somewhat downcast. Several times, she shifted her position in her seat. She breathed a bit faster and irregularly. Finally, she looked up from the pages and closed her eyes. She tilted her face upward and slowly moved her head from side to side as if to say, "This isn't right." Or, "I can't believe it."

I didn't yet know what she was thinking or feeling, but I was certain that the assessment results and examples had hit their target. This time she didn't explain how wrong she thought everyone else was. Instead, she spoke in brief quiet phrases that seemed to come from some unfamiliar place deep inside.

"They just...don't know me."

"If only they knew...how much...I care about...each of them...and for our organization."

She slowly poured out a litany of laments that could only come from someone who felt so misunderstood, so often, and for so long.

That was the beginning of our work together. For the next year, her journey meandered through work on her *Identity*. She gave full and unedited voice to the part of her that felt misunderstood and, more importantly, to the part of her that defended that misunderstood part. These two sub-personalities worked like a tag team. They hijacked most of Elizabeth's energy when she interacted with other people, and they interpreted most dealings as assaults.

She had to first become aware how often she had perceived these interactions as intentional injuries. As she expanded her awareness of both her own and of other's internal processes, she began to interact with others in ways that didn't call in her defender part—the part that habitually lashed out and bullied others whenever there was the slightest provocation. Finally, she also became aware that it simply wasn't all about her parts and their reactions. Others had parts too.

Through the year of our work together, Elizabeth discovered how her unique personality had formed in response to her early life circumstances. Her father died when she was eight years old, and over the next several years, her mother became increasingly unable to cope with the burden of single parenting. In order for her younger siblings to receive the security and order they needed and deserved, Elizabeth, the oldest of four children, picked up many of the household roles vacated by her parents.

Her defender part and her director part were both needed in those early days of her life; they were necessary for her situation. Now, those primary sub-personalities, which were needed while she was still a young girl, began to overwhelm her developing sense of self as an adolescent.

As she became a teenager and young adult, her view of the world was primarily seen through the lens of these two parts. She perceived many interactions in her personal life as a threat, and by doing so, her defender jumped in to guard her and others. Then her director part joined in to vanquish those who seemed threatening. From time to time, these traits were rewarded in her career development even though she also carried the liabilities of these unmanaged parts. This pattern continued until the day when her defenses crumbled before the powerful, yet kind, directness of her manager and her peers.

Then, as our work together progressed and she understood her own sub-personalities more, she began to see how other people's parts collided with hers in certain flashpoints at work. She was then able to mobilize her inner maestro to direct more appropriate responses. During this process, she became aware of the options she had for dealing with her own emotions and with those of her co-workers.

She slowly began to approach situations with curiosity and optimism rather than fear or aggression. This change then made room for her other parts that were generous and wise. She came to see that others were fighting their own battles as well, and she began to understand and empathize with the circumstances that had built and strengthened other people's unconscious and sometimes out-of-control sub-personalities.

What was the path Elizabeth took to increase her *Capacity for Connection* with others?

Insight—Capacity For Connection

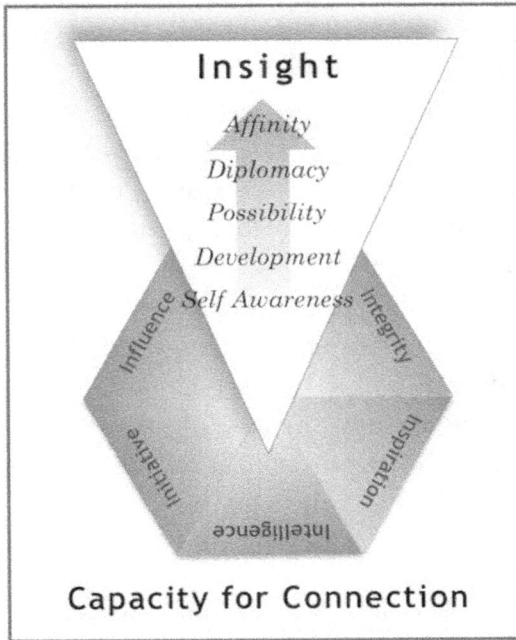

By its very meaning, *Insight* is an inward facing phenomenon. Elizabeth initiated her call for help because of the complications of living with only an outward focus. In our work together, she became aware that she lacked a deep understanding of others and how her own drives and actions affected them.

Too many leaders are only outward looking, forcing their own agenda onto events and people with little apparent awareness of their own personhood. Although, since you're reading this, you almost certainly already value the personal benefits of a keen *Insight*. Yet there are some who like to mock the efforts of others to gain *Insight*, and they say it's merely self-centered naval gazing. And I agree—in part.

I've met a few individuals whose inner journey seemed to be a slow inward spiral with only their own interests positioned perfectly at the center. If all you can see is "you" at the center, you have not looked at or answered the second *Identity* question: Why are you here? None of the people I've met who had only "me" at their center were ever leaders. Nor were they likely to ever become leaders unless they transformed like Elizabeth did.

Even though most of us acknowledge that *Insight* is a beneficial attribute, we're a bit uncomfortable with psychology. And almost all of us would probably describe *Insight* as being very personal, deeply interior, occasionally embarrassing or even painful yet potentially awesome, and possibly magical.

This journey to becoming a leader reminds me of what mountaineer Chis Kalman said after he was forced to forego his greatest climbing dream, the arduous ascent in the Torres del Paine National Park in southern Chilean Patagonia. Instead, he was called to fulfill an important and pressing family obligation at home in the flatlands of Maryland.

> I'm reminded that the greatest challenge is not to travel abroad but to travel within, not to conquer unclimbed routes on remote walls of sheer stone, but to seek out seldom visited terrain in one's heart, mind, and soul. In short, to push oneself to improve when improving proves most trying. And while they may not be as tempestuous as the Torres, our inner landscapes are just as intimidating, just as breathtaking, and without a doubt, just as rewarding to behold.[1]

As you expand *Insight,* your *Capacity For Connection,* you'll certainly travel into your interior, and yet the core of your psyche will not be your final destination. Rather, the purpose of expanding your *Insight* is to reach out to connect deeply with others in a mutually significant way. *Insight* brings the ability to care about "other"—not just other people but all that is outside of you. This capacity links you with both people and planet. This *Capacity for Connection* arises in stages from *Self-Awareness,* grows through attention to your *Development,* possesses an attitude of *Possibility,* conducts itself with *Diplomacy,* and matures into a deep *Affinity* for all life.

Let's begin the journey of connecting-to-other by starting at home—within yourself.

Self-Awareness

Self-Awareness is the profound understanding, acceptance, and appreciation of your own complexity. This stage of building the capacity of *Insight* is important for each of us, but it is a critical stage for the evolving leader who is seeking to interact well with others.

As you read in the chapter on *Identity,* you not only have your own sub-personalities at play, but you must be simultaneously aware of yourself *while* you're playing your parts. Central to this awareness is your ability to discover and direct the appropriate functions of your personality—to conduct your own orchestra. By doing this, you first help yourself and then you benefit others. Without this *Self-Awareness,* you toss your inner distortions outwardly onto others because you keep thinking that others are the cause of your difficulties.

Self-Awareness is not just the discouraging realization of your internal faults. It is also the thrill of recognizing your unlimited possibilities. In this stage you're invited to act responsibly about your weaknesses, as well as your strengths.

Only then can your potential flourish like Elizabeth's did. She had huge blind spots about how her actions affected others, and this blindness impaired her potential for a mutually valued relationship with her colleagues.

Seeing the information gathered from an assessment, similar to the format that I used with Elizabeth, is similar to viewing a video of your golf swing or a video of the presentation you made at the annual sales meeting. Seeing and hearing yourself through the experience that others have of you is a rare and valuable perspective. We most often only see ourselves through our own already filtered self-perception. However, merely finding out what others think about you will not change your *Self-Awareness*. The process also requires acceptance of the truth about you followed by dedicated and corrective action.

Elizabeth had reached a point in her career, and in her life, where she finally cared about how she was perceived. She finally *wanted* to change; she wanted to take actions that would result in changing herself.

In my experience, two factors promote *Self-Awareness*. One is an *external* stimulus; when a person receives repeated feedback from others that significantly differs from one's self-perspective—like the feedback Elizabeth received from her colleagues. The other factor occurs from an *internal* conflict: when one of your sub-personal parts bristles in opposition to the actions of another one of your parts and you're pressured to mediate the situation.

What will you do with the awareness you gain, regardless of where it comes from? How does your capacity of *Insight* expand? And what occurs internally—within the terrain that is your inner landscape? Like Elizabeth, this is when many leaders reach outside of themselves for help. Some talk to a trusted peer, others seek a coach or a minister, still others click onto Amazon and buy some books. Regardless of your next step, the process of gaining *Insight* will require you to explore the next four stages as well.

Development

As your *Self-Awareness* evolves, you'll soon face the choice of what you should do with the new information about yourself. As the reader, you're undoubtedly already inclined toward your own growth and personal enhancement. Nonetheless, you should know that with *Self-Awareness* comes a kind of vigilance, meaning that what you now know cannot be un-known, you cannot fall back asleep. In this way, a perpetual unfolding of deeper levels of awareness is available to you if you take on your inner domain with the same attention that you give to developing your organizational enterprise.

In moments of weary exhaustion or of aching muscles from the heavy lifting required to pull yourself together, you might resort to the old repetitions of more primitive behaviors. "Hey, I can't be expected to be perfect all the time, can I?" Or as one of my clients said with deliberate irony, "There are so many levels of self-awareness and so many benefits in each level, it's endless. It's the gift that keeps on giving."

Adopting a *Development* attitude, and thereby expanding your *Insight*, is similar to any other cutting edge area of your life. In the same way that New Years' resolutions and gym memberships soar in January and plummet in February, you will either hit the snooze button on your newly found *Self-Awareness*, or you will push against the warm-bed-inertia and awaken. Remember that all of this is still happening within your own mind; no one else can see or hear the debate among your parts. You have the option to choose to get up and to show up—or not. Your emerging inclination toward *Development* occurs as you begin to be less self-centered. You are coming out of your shell and are less likely to become captivated by the wonders you discover about yourself.

How does this inclination towards *Development* occur? What are the circumstances that increase your chances of becoming a leader rather than remaining at the level of manager or even "boss"?

I've already discussed some of these early internal factors when I introduced sub-personalities back in chapter 2, *Identity*. But let's look at this from a slightly different perspective. Let's look at early childhood. What are some possible internal influencers that cause a child to look outward with a different mindset—one that leads toward growth vs. stasis? Why do some people thrive when faced with a challenge while others thrash against the obstacles or even give up and turn away?

Stanford University researcher and psychologist Carol Dweck discovered something remarkable in the various ways children reacted to the same challenge. Some avoided the challenge while others actually loved being faced with the potential failure that a challenge could bring. The latter group seemed to know "that human qualities, such as intellectual skills, could be cultivated. And that's what they were doing—getting smarter. Not only weren't they discouraged by failure, they didn't even think they were failing. They thought they were *learning* [emphasis added]."[2]

Dweck posits two mindsets, "fixed" vs. "growth," as a way to understand how people differ. Somewhere among our many life circumstances, some of us make a choice to see our performance as either succeeding or failing. By resorting to this viewpoint, we fall into a *fixed* mindset. Except Dweck discovered that the children she was studying had not yet made the binary choice between success and failure. They were operating with a third option—a growth mindset. They were *learning*.

It's possible that you might just be one of these *learning* individuals. And this is where the age-old debate about nature vs. nurture enters. Is it genes, or is it environment that shape our human differences? Throughout history the predominant thinking has tilted in one direction or the other.

Today most experts recognize that both factors ultimately create the person.

Except, there's another twist to this calculation. It turns out that this *both/and* explanation of human development is also inadequate because there appears to also be a secret sauce in the mix. People who purposefully develop themselves demonstrate this distinction. It's their attitude.

Dweck adds, "This growth mindset is based on the belief that your basic qualities are things you can cultivate through your efforts, your strategies, and help from others. Although people may differ in every which way—in their initial talents and aptitudes, interests, or temperaments—everyone can change and grow through application and experience."[3]

The difference in the children Dweck studied and in the most effective and mature leaders we see today, as well as throughout history, is the same "secret sauce": a growth mindset.

Or as leadership guru, Warren Bennis, says, "Leaders wonder about everything, want to learn as much as they can, are willing to take risks, experiment, try new things. They do not worry about failure, but embrace errors, knowing they will learn from them. True leaders are not born, but made, and usually self-made. Leaders invent themselves."[4]

Though you may find such attention to growth to be demanding, a clear sense of self will help you to avoid being brought down by the forces of your sub-personalities—your parts that seem to operate without regard for the larger interests of your life and purpose. Hence it's a combined effort; you'll require both awareness and determination to develop *Insight*. And Bennis reminds us, "Developing character and vision is the way leaders invent themselves."[5]

While the "secret sauce" is bubbling on the inside, there are also outside factors that affect your *Development*. Some of your early influencers included your home, school, and eventually your workplace. Potential leaders blossom when working within an organization that already believes that people can grow and can change for the better. These organizations value a structure and a process for increasing the complex learning options for their employees. And these organizations search out *potential* talent rather than merely hire and promote *natural* and obvious talent.

Though this book focuses on you, the individual, we also must look at the impact organizations have on human development since they're such a significant part of our societies. Study after study has shown that organizations that place a high value on continually developing their people into valued and satisfied leaders rise to the top in many other beneficial metrics as well. One report by research firm Bersin & Associates summed it up this way: "Leadership development is not just about developing leaders, it is about creating a culture of accountability and performance. Leadership development creates a magnet for high-performers and fosters a high-performance organization. That is why organizations that are 'built to last' have strong histories of leadership development."[6]

You might be one of the fortunate ones who have been supported by a home, a school, or a working environment that believed *more* was possible through your progress. Some organizations embody this mindset that people can fulfill their potential. Sadly, others are either ignorant of this possibility, or worse, choose to limit human potential in favor of some other supposedly expedient goal.

When I've had the privilege to consult with some yet-to-become leaders, my counsel to them has always been to seek out those companies, or teams within their existing organization, that have a clear and committed track record for developing their people.

With the growth you experience through this stage of *Development*, you'll now inevitably move on to the next stage of *Insight*.

Possibility

Leaders with a mindset toward growth now effortlessly advance into the next stage in this *Capacity for Connection, Possibility*. As you develop, you're naturally exploring your potential to go into the unknown and to discover how to act in this new place.

In my work with executives, one exercise I use to informally gauge a client's capacity for *Insight* is to suggest that they do something a bit unusual for them; like tryout with a local improvisation theater club, or audition for a role in a community theater, or run a 10k race, or even write poetry. I usually propose an activity that I suspect will be outside their comfort zone.

I'm frequently amazed at the hesitant reactions I get to these ideas. You're probably thinking that you'd also be resistant. Just remember that your task as a leader is to find the wherewithal to go where others hesitate, to venture forward without a map, and to guide others into territory that may not yet be familiar.

When you engage in an unfamiliar task, notice how open or closed and fearful you are to experimenting with the unknown. *Possibility* is all about the sensations, experiences, places, and thoughts you have on your journey toward some goal. Loosen up, lean back, breathe in, and smile as you unpack your gear (including a note-taking journal so you can document your progress on all levels) and start enjoying the trip ahead into the unknown and towards a possible future.

At this mid-point in expanding your capacity of *Insight*, you'll notice that the process of your expansion begins to break through your skin—it is no longer only an invisible, internal, and private matter. Your *Insight* now becomes externalized. *Possibility* implies that something is about to be birthed out of you. Similar to a seed, you will at some point emerge from hidden internal activity and sprout into the surrounding environment.

Others might notice that you're venturing forth when they would've hesitated. A wise and trusted mentor, if you have one, will certainly notice the telltale sprouting of your *Possibility*. Elizabeth achieved this metamorphosis as she steadfastly stared in the face of the pain of her own sprouting. She saw herself as someone who could change, as someone who was good, and as someone who already had the seed of authentic leadership inside. And I have to believe that her supervisor also saw this potential in her, or he would not have invested in her as he did.

She began to see herself as someone who could become something that she had never imagined. She actually experienced her own *Possibility* similarly to how the philosopher, Rousseau, described it when he said, "The bounds of human possibility are not as confining as we think they are; they are made to seem to be tight by our weaknesses, our vices, our prejudices that confine them."[7]

To develop *Possibility,* you will need to approach situations with curiosity and optimism. You can't be constrained by fear or by acting with aggression. When you remain open to what can happen, or to what is possible, you are living out of a confidence in your own self as well as a trust that others have the seed of *Possibility* within themselves as well.

Mahatma Gandhi, a leader who certainly embodied *Possibility*, said, "Man often becomes what he believes himself to be. If I keep on saying to myself that I cannot do a certain thing, it is possible that I may end by really becoming incapable of doing it. On the contrary, if I have the belief that I can do it, I shall surely acquire the capacity to do it even if I may not have it at the beginning."[8]

During the 1980's and 1990's, many sidewalk philosophers circulated an unrealistically optimistic view, a view that echoed Dr. Norman Vincent Peale's philosophy of positive thinking. The idea was that if you spoke affirmations to yourself regularly (e.g., "I am patient and loving") you would eventually realize the desired state. While many psychologists have found value in holding an optimistic mindset, there are an equal number who debunk these approaches.

There is a huge problem with announcing a possibility as if it was already an accomplished state. And that's because it is simply not true. Affirmations are different from visions, as we'll explore in chapter 5, because affirmations can cause a rift in one's awareness. There can be a battle of your sub-personalities about what is true and what isn't. The rift consumes the energy that would otherwise give birth to *Insight*. But the upside to envisioning a possibility is that you are more likely to experience the desired state than if you simply wait for fate, luck, or some other coincidence to show up.

Parker Palmer, Quaker elder, educator, and activist, describes how to truthfully look at the future even when the present is undesirable.

> In my own life, as my winters segue into spring, I find it not only hard to cope with mud but also hard to credit the small harbingers of larger life to come, hard to hope until the outcome is secure. Spring teaches me to look more carefully for the green stems of possibility: for the intuitive hunch that may turn into a larger insight, for the glance or touch that may thaw a frozen relationship, for the stranger's act of kindness that makes the world seem hospitable again.[9]

Possibility becomes reality when we attend to it. Where is your attention? One thing is certain; as you expand your *Capacity for Connection* you'll engage differently with others. What is possible for you in your leading?

Diplomacy

In this stage, *Diplomacy*, you'll improve your capability to relate with others because you have become intimately acquainted with your own inner human landscape, and therefore, you sense what is also going on inside other people.

Diplomacy means that you manage your behavior in a way that is reassuring to others rather than causing them to have uncertainty and fear. More importantly, it means that you can see another's potential, while at the same time, you're aware of the likely obstacles they'll encounter before experiencing success. You'll need to employ a highly perceptive stage of *Diplomacy* in order to become a judicious and effective leader. And since you're now aware of your own inner tendencies, you can more fully empathize with others in your common predicament of merely being human.

This level of understanding of both yourself and another is powerful since it prepares you for engaging in all kinds of negotiations. Being *Diplomatic* provides a kind of invisible shield against the personal attacks that another may launch at you because they're still attached to one of their threatened sub-personalities. As an Inside*OUT* leader, you know that their reactivity is a throwback to a set of behaviors that served them in earlier times. *Diplomacy* implies that you don't take affronts personally. You know that the aggressor is really expressing self-statements, even though many of the pronouns might be directed at you. When you're faced with blame for alleged errors, you can discern between allegations that are merely the projections of a wounded attacker and those that actually should lie at your feet as the leader. It takes a calm and clear head to first make this distinction, then to keep from derailing the conversation, and finally to strategize a beneficial direction.

Remember how Elizabeth acted before her capacity for *Diplomacy* emerged? She experienced other's differing opinions and actions as intentional attacks. Although, as she became more aware of her own part in interactions, she learned how to reinterpret those events in ways that didn't evoke her defender part. She slowly became aware that it simply wasn't all about her.

In this way, *Diplomacy* is a lot like empathy. As you become more and more conscious of your own parts and the roles they play in your life, you'll become more receptive to the complexity of others. This means that you'll not be stalled at only having *Self-Awareness,* but you'll have more resources available for how you can respond and you'll be able to move forward in your actions with full consideration of the other person. You'll also be able to perceive if the other person is operating with *Self-Awareness* or may just be acting from the level of one of their sub-personalities. By using *Diplomacy*, you'll be able to reach a solution that's more agreeable to both parties.

However, many leaders fail the *Diplomacy* test when there's a crisis or some other need for immediate action. They often resort to a go-it-alone attitude. In critical moments, such as when having to handle unforeseen surprises, leaders could take some clues from another type of organization and their leaders: expeditions. Both organizational leaders and expeditionary leaders require vision, planning, cooperation, and dealing with contingencies. But expeditions are different from organizations because they are severely time compressed and environmentally stressed enterprises. So, when physical conditions are intensified, both expeditions and organizations do not have the luxury of time and space to deal with unforeseen events. They must act skillfully and immediately.

In a private conversation I had with explorer and environmental scientist, Tim Jarvis, who in 2013 led an Antarctic adventure to recreate the last portion of the 1915-16 Shackleton expedition, he said, "Today, the boss, as Shackleton was affectionately called, would be referred to as a leader with emotional intelligence. But what I didn't expect was that I would also need to be a similar source of strength for my team."[10]

Jarvis knew, like Shackleton before him, that all expedition decisions were ultimately his own; he also realized that under incredibly stressful and dangerous conditions success inevitably requires a deft hand in dealing with others. After all, Jarvis was also a seasoned Antarctic pioneer. In 1999, he had undertaken "what many regard as one of the last great land-based challenges on earth—crossing the continent's 2,700 kilometers on foot and unsupported [while] pulling a sled weighing 225 kilograms through obstructive icy terrain."[11]

Though Jarvis' journey ended prematurely due to a fuel contaminated food supply, he did learn how to deal with unexpected adversity and to deal with it immediately. Similarly, once Shackleton's ship became unexpectedly icebound, he didn't wait until he needed to abandon their sinking ship before he put his survival plan into action. Jarvis described how Shackleton had used his knowledge of himself and his men to prepare for their journey. "Now the eccentricities of his recruitment process came to the fore: the optimism and flexibility he had looked for in each man began to pay dividends. Shackleton held optimism almost above all else, calling it 'true moral courage,' and they would need all they had to get through."[12]

In *Chasing Shackleton*, the account of his daring and successful reenactment, Jarvis said, "[Shackleton's] care of his men and determination to keep spirits up were indefatigable, and his ability to maintain his optimism in the face of seemingly insurmountable odds now struck me more forcefully than ever. By comparison I was faced with relatively minor discontent and doubt among my team."[13]

What stands out to me is how both Jarvis and Shackleton exhibited their capacities of *Diplomacy* during really tough ordeals. They both had the capacity to consider each team member's physical, mental, and emotional states in their decision-making processes. And what drove both of these expedition leaders when making alterations to the course of their endeavors was their intent that each man survives and returns safely to his family.

Diplomacy performed in significantly more physical comfort, but no less demanding circumstances, is the example of former Senator George Mitchell's efforts to shepherd a peace process in Northern Ireland. In a 2007 interview with *The Guardian,* he said, "Over time what happened was that because there was so much controversy and difficulty getting started I really served as a neutral arbiter, more like a judge which I had been before. I think they began to gain some confidence that I would act in a fair and impartial way. Indeed over time I established what I believed were quite good personal and cordial relations with all of the parties, including those who had been opposed to my participation."[14]

These examples of *Diplomacy* show just a few ways that this capacity is revealed in leadership. These individuals had honed their skills, their thinking, and their sensitivities in real-world environments. They didn't do everything perfectly, and their endeavors were fraught with mishaps. While their interactions with others were not always flawless, they approached the people who worked with them with a dignity and respect borne of familiarity with their own foibles. And they earned the commitment of their followers by interacting honestly, respectfully, and fairly—ways that all humans want to be treated.

While *Diplomacy* involves the skill for handling matters without arousing hostility, it also includes an awareness of organizational dynamics and an understanding of how individuals and groups affect each other. Once you've developed your *Capacity For Connection* to this level, you're ready to balance the needs of individuals with those of larger ecosystems, be they social, commercial, or environmental.

Affinity

This stage, *Affinity*, is a state we long for. Except it's more like a summit that, when standing at Base Camp, might seem impossible to reach. Yet most of us don't dwell at the summit. Instead we often trek around on paths well below but always mindful of one day standing on the summit.

After all the work you did in the previous stages to expand your capacity for *Insight*, you're now operating with a deeper connection to others, and you possess an aroused heart of compassion for all life. You care for your organization, community, and planet as if it were your life—because it is!

And here, your regard for yourself expresses outwardly as a genuine love for all beings *and* for the planet. *Affinity* means that you're protecting a place for all life on the planet and relating to the entire world in a way that honors the intricate web of all life.

In a recent TED talk, anthropologist and Buddhist teacher Joan Halifax summed it up this way. "...A line that the Dalai Lama once said, 'Love and compassion are necessities. They're not luxuries. Without them, humanity cannot survive.' And I would suggest it is not only humanity that won't survive, but it is all species on the planet... It is the big cats and it's the plankton."[15]

Unfortunately, many corporate leaders seem to collapse when it comes to *Affinity*. Their failure is most likely due to incomplete development in an earlier stage and a lack of integration of the development afforded in the other capacities. Their actions reveal that they choose to connect more deeply with their shareholders' demands and their own financial security than to promote the welfare of our entire ecosystem. In doing so, they abandon true security and all they actually cherish in exchange for prestige and power. Can you imagine what our businesses, our nation, and even our world would be like if our leaders actually acted out of compassion for all that is?

In the 1990's, we almost never heard words like "spirit" or "soul" used in connection with "corporate" or "business." Yet there were many who were wrestling to find a vernacular for describing what they believed to be a deep moral crisis in our society. Eventually, writers like Peter Senge and Warren Bennis (to name just two of many) found the right words that described the predicament and in doing so aroused the energy and courage of other leaders' to create a new day in organizations. Max DePree, former CEO at the Herman Miller office furniture company, led his organization in ways that reflected his caring values and then wrote many books on leadership so more of us could be influenced by his heart and mind.

Another leader who contributed to the proliferation of writings about spirit in the workplace is Bill George, formerly the CEO at Medtronic and more recently a senior fellow at Harvard Business School. He has authored several books and continues to shape our perspectives on enlightened leadership by his frequent appearances on CNBC and in his blog posts.

Many writers have used notions like transformation, values, and even quantum physics to capture our attention, educate us, and point us toward *Affinity*. One of the most sweeping yet intelligible books I ever read that described leadership and organizational development is Margaret Wheatley's, *Leadership and the New Science*. For me, her logical and inspiring explanations connect science to real world business and take me to the threshold of mystery.

In addition to our spirits becoming aroused, the term "social responsibility" started to show up in business discourse. Some leaders used this term as the rails on which to roll strong ethical values into their organizations. Many leaders who embraced social responsibility not only created a significant impact on local and global issues, but they also achieved remarkable financial successes. By 2010, the International Organization for Standardization (ISO) developed their ISO 26000 to help organizations effectively assess and address social responsibilities that were relevant and significant to the following: their mission and vision; their operations and processes; their people including customers, employees, communities, and other stakeholders; and their environmental impact.

Today, many companies are keen to tell their corporate social responsibility (CSR) stories on their websites or on product displays and hang tags. Some even become activist organizations, like Ben & Jerry's, that, in addition, just happen to design, manufacture, and sell products. Every time I hear Yvon Chouinard describe how and why he started Patagonia, I hear a sage giving counsel to others who'd be prudent to follow. He says that he never wanted to be a businessman. All he wanted to do was to do his craft and climb mountains. Eventually he had to figure out how to be a businessman but to do it completely on his own terms: build the best products, cause no unnecessary harm, and inspire and invent solutions to the environmental crisis.

As I reflect about highly visible leaders and their organizations, several other companies immediately pop into mind: Stonyfield Farm, Timberland, Google, and Toms Shoes are just a few. And I bet you can also think of some because we are now showered with branding messages that promote many companies' socially valuable contributions.

Bob Rosen, a trusted CEO advisor, talks about the formula for this kind of endeavor in his book, *Grounded*. "Businesses who embrace corporate social responsibility (CSR) are aware that commercial success cannot be considered separately from a broader context of respect for community, people and planet. The concept is best expressed as the formula: social responsibility = higher purpose + global connectedness + generosity of spirit."[16]

Affinity requires you to have an open heart borne of keen understanding. It is not simply a sentimental type of caring, but a deep affection for others. As an Inside*OUT* leader, you guide others who seek to learn about their own impact on their environment and those in it. You aim to nurture the latent potential in all people. Yet those you touch are not the only beneficiaries of your *Affinity*. You benefit as well; you gain emotional, mental, and physical health. I contend that you, by expanding your *Capacity for Connection*, will also build enduring relationships that create longevity and happiness for yourself.

One proof of the benefit you'll receive is the Harvard Study of Adult Development that has tracked the lives of 724 men for seventy-eight years. Robert Waldinger, the director of the study, wrote.

> Good relationships keep us happier and healthier. Period. We've learned three big lessons about relationship. The first is that social connections are really good for us, and that loneliness kills. The second big lesson that we learned is that it's not just the number of friends you have, and it's not whether or not you're in a committed relationship, but it's the quality of your close relationships that matters. The third big lesson that we learned about relationships and our health is that good relationships don't just protect our bodies, they protect our brains.[17]

This discussion on *Insight—the Capacity for Connection—* started by looking inward and ended up by facing outward. In the end, it's the relationships that you foster that will enhance the happiness in your own life. This capacity is succinctly stated in the Seventh Principle that guides the members of Unitarian Universalist congregations. They affirm and promote "respect for the interdependent web of all existence of which we are a part."

Businesses, communities, and societies are simply complex extensions of the same aspects found within each person. Consequently, in this era of social media and instant information, we must all lean toward leaders who cherish their *Capacity for Connection* on a truly global and planetary scale.

Parker Palmer reminds us that, "Citizenship is a way of being in the world rooted in the knowledge that I am a member of a vast community of human and nonhuman beings that I depend on for essentials I could never provide for myself."[18]

Coda

When I last spoke to Elizabeth, she told me what she had accomplished by putting her maestro in charge of her previously unmanaged parts. She was spearheading a company-wide initiative to train each employee to communicate more effectively. The key personal take-away for her from these training programs was that she now waits before expressing her own opinion until after she understands what the other person said, from their point of view. Being the company's sponsor of this initiative gave her the chance to really think about, talk about, and practice these skills herself.

Then she got the chance to observe and manage her well-honed sensitivities to protect. The CEO appointed her to be the leader of an organization-wide task force to develop a "zero-waste" initiative—no small project for this global manufacturing giant. When we spoke, she said that the largest assembly plant in the U.S. was already 75% successful. And she no longer needed my help.

The supreme quality for leadership is unquestionably integrity. Without it, no real success is possible, no matter whether it is on a section gang, a football field, in an army, or in an office.

—Dwight D. Eisenhower

4

INTEGRITY
Capacity for Transparency

Peter

When Peter met me in baggage claim at San Francisco International Airport, I felt an immediate ease with him. His voice was calm, he had pleasant yet slightly mischievous eyes, and his laughter rippled out in a most disarming way. He grabbed one of my bags as he said something about a very short walk to where he parked his car. The late afternoon California sunshine angled into our eyes as we dodged the cars exiting the garage.

During our walk to the car, he asked about my flight and if I was tired from the cross-continent flight. I assured him that I still had a large dose of adrenalin going for me and that I would be good for another several hours. That seemed to satisfy him because he immediately suggested that we have dinner at one of his favorite area restaurants.

An Audi A8, huh? At least he was maintaining the appearance of success. The door locks chirped, headlights flashed, the mirrors deployed, and after we loaded my bags into the auto-open/auto-close rear hatch, we slid into the caramel-colored leather seats. Hey, these seats are so much more comfortable than the economy class seat I was molded into for the previous five hours.

Peter was a third-generation CEO of an international consulting group, inheriting the firm from his father, Frank. Peter's grandfather, the founder, was quite a social entrepreneur. In the 1960s, while his comrades were despising those "hippies" and "street people" and calling them "malcontents," Peter's grandfather was convinced these kids were the vanguard of a huge social change when he launched Apex Partners. Among the consulting staff, there were former businesspeople, a few psychology professors, some former schoolteachers, and even a few former clergy. It must have seemed like some kind of halfway house for professional eccentrics.

Nonetheless, Grandfather was onto something. He recruited for a certain quality of individual and sought them from a range of careers. He was a great admirer of W. Edwards Deming who had worked on the quality movement in post-WWII Japan. Grandfather believed that Deming's philosophy of continual improvement could also be applied to organizations and not only to manufacturing processes. By both becoming more responsive to their employees' needs and dreams and by championing social and environmental awareness, Grandfather believed that corporations could become vital social forces.

Peter reminisced how his grandfather had always talked wistfully about the 1967 Summer of Love and the 1969 Woodstock Festival claiming that, more than any politician, those events shaped the succeeding 50 years of change and awareness in the U.S.

Apex was a very successful consulting firm whose principal consultants also authored papers and published business/organizational books. It was renowned in the training and development field for its breakthrough approaches to the people side of the business. Apex created and conducted seminars around the world. They built a leadership center where managers and executives gathered to study and hone their craft. Their key component in all this work was their approach to bringing out the best in people. Apex had its largest presence in the U.S., but it also had a reputation and assignments in Asia and Europe.

The company had its most significant growth under the leadership of Peter's dad, Frank. However, Apex had plateaued since Frank had turned the reigns over to his son, Peter. Along with the company, and the corner office, Peter inherited his dad's and his grandfather's ideals of serving the greater good and caring deeply for "their people."

After our dinner arrived, Peter finally came to the real issue. He was deeply troubled about something, and that was why he had wanted my input. Perhaps, if his organization manufactured widgets or even operated a fleet of moving vans, he might not have been troubled, at least not now. Now he had uncovered a nasty history about his dad, Frank, and he needed to clean house.

During Frank's tenure as CEO, he had behaved in ways that were counter to the values embodied by Apex. For example, Frank would on occasion viciously berate an employee in front of others for what appeared to be the slightest challenge to his authority or ideas. After Peter took over, he discovered that even though Frank had retired there was still a black cloud hanging over the company. In addition, some current personnel were planning to go public with Frank's moral inconsistencies.

Here was an organization that was a beacon for integrity in business relations. The keystone approach that the company employed and promoted was "to seek to understand" the other party in any conversation—especially those interactions that were emotionally loaded. Frank had authored papers on the topic. Other internal consultants had written books on best business practices that focused on human communication. Now Peter was faced with emerging details that could ruin the organization if he didn't skillfully handle the situation.

Another wrinkle involved the Board of Directors. Frank had selected most of the members. During the previous two decades, they had all put "growing the organization" ahead of the behaviors they taught. They had succeeded and profited, and now, Peter feared the Board would become edgy and defensive about any questions that zeroed in on his dad's behavior.

Peter openly admitted to me that he wondered if Frank and the Board had been complicit. He questioned whether they already knew the things about his dad that he, Peter, had only recently discovered. He feared he might stumble and fall on a minefield of potentially worse discoveries. He also feared his own short fuse, which was likely to get triggered while cleaning up this potentially lethal corporate secret.

Integrity—Capacity for Transparency

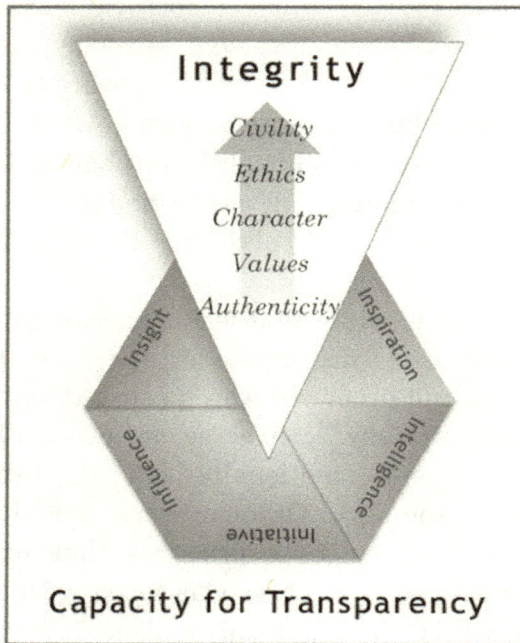

Integrity means you have nothing to hide. By developing this capacity, you become someone who people describe using phrases like "she walks the talk," or "he's true to the core." Transparency means that the person others see on the surface is the same person through and through. As you'll discover in this chapter, your values as an Inside*OUT* leader will be on display in all your interactions. Your *Capacity for Transparency* cannot contain deceit, manipulation, or political gamesmanship. And just in case you're wondering, being transparent does not automatically give you permission to use unkind candor.

Being transparent does not imply that you give a free pass to your less mature parts. You're still expected to have your inner maestro do the leading.

Transparency means you tell the truth even when it's difficult to do so, and you act kindly, which might be even more difficult. As we discovered in the chapter on *Insight*, you always need to consider the receiver. *Integrity* also implies that you are willing to have others question your motives and methods, and yet, you remain present even when others misunderstand you.

We admire individuals like Nelson Mandela, Mother Theresa, Dietrich Bonhoeffer, Sallie Krawcheck, Dan Bane, Indra Nooyi, Malala Yousafzai, the Dalai Lama, and many other leaders, past and present, for their moral stance. This doesn't mean that they are perfect or that they've not failed in some rather public ways. At the same time, each of them exemplifies an obvious moral foundation in their positions and decisions.

Then there are those who would not even make the moral leader list. When leaders slip, fail, or display a disingenuous characteristic, we usually remember them for their errors and forget any admirable qualities they might have had. It's as if their better selves never existed. We see this when political leaders who promote "family values" are simultaneously unfaithful to their partners, candidates who promise healthcare for all and then once in office vote very differently, or Olympic coaches who violate the sacred trust placed in them by parents and by youthful athletes. Unfortunately, leaders who violate our trust often become more highly visible than those leaders who faithfully go about their work.

As Parker Palmer says, "A leader is someone with the power to project either shadow or light onto some part of the world and onto the lives of the people who dwell there. A leader shapes the ethos in which others must live, an ethos as light-filled as heaven or as shadowy as hell. A good leader is intensely aware of the interplay of inner shadow and light, lest the act of leadership do more harm than good."[1]

What does it take for you to be a person of moral fiber *and* nerves of steel when facing the daunting pressures of organizational leadership?

To become a leader with a highly developed *Capacity for Transparency*, first you enter the stage of *Authenticity*. Then you will expand through the stage of *Values* and the certainty of your *Character*. Your continued transparent interactions with others results in the stage of *Ethics*, and ultimately *Integrity's* full expression is in the stage of *Civility*, which means that as a leader you create organizations where trust and truth become the currencies of your commerce across the board.

Authenticity

Your answers to the key questions about your *Identity*— who am I, why am I here, and where am I going—position you for this stage in your development. You've already considered those deep questions about yourself and by doing so have begun to change the person you perceive yourself to be to the person you really are.

Your further development in this stage of *Authenticity* is another opening through which your inner world eventually gets projected onto your community. You'll need your inner maestro to show up for the performance, not a subpersonality with its clamoring to be heard and pounding its fist inside your head. You have to do your inner work first and to do it well so you can embody the entire capacity of *Integrity*.

Psychologist author, Nina Burrowes says it so clearly.

Authenticity is a concept often discussed in the workplace, especially when it comes to leadership. Today when people use the term 'authenticity' they usually mean that they are being honest and open. To be an authentic leader is to be genuine.

If you want to understand the true meaning of authenticity you need to go back to its root. The Latin root of the word 'authenticity' is 'author', so being 'authentic' doesn't mean being honest about who you are, it's about being your own 'author'. Authenticity is an active and creative process. It's not about revealing something, it's about building something; and that something is 'you'.

If you want to be authentic in the workplace, don't focus on revealing who you are, instead focus on creating and truly becoming yourself.[2]

When you're centered within yourself, you're aware of whether you're truly forging your own being or whether you're just conforming to the pressures of others. *Authenticity* is when you feel most deeply and intensely you, not someone else's idea of you. American philosopher and psychologist William James once described this genuine experience as the inner voice saying, "This is the real me."

Because this inner domain is unseen by others, you must have a coherent sense of self to discern *which* inner voice is speaking. You cannot depend on friends or colleagues to point out something they cannot see. When Peter learned about his dad's moral inconsistencies, he could have simply looked straight ahead and ignored the effects of his dad's past behavior. He could have gone with the flow of one of the voices in his head that reminded him to not make waves, the voice that also reminded him that he had a pretty cushy job and not to jeopardize his career.

However, Peter borrowed a page from William James' writings and stepped into his real self. He began to expand his capacity for *Integrity* the moment he listened to his maestro and decided to confront his dad's disingenuous behaviors and the ways dad had tainted the company.

Meanwhile, if you've read and worked on your *Identity— Capacity for Self-Mastery,* you've already done the heavy lifting required for expanding yourself, and now you're more capable of authoring yourself rather than simply 'being honest' as **Burrowes** just reminded us.

Even though you might see yourself as having lifted yourself up by your own bootstraps (wow, picture that) or as being a self-made individual, you probably should examine the source of your claim. Declarations like these are insufficient to describe all of the elements that shape any person, let alone those that form the foundations of a leader. So pause and consider. Is this the real you speaking, or is it one of your dominant subpersonalities?

While many leaders have been shaped through epic self-effort, few, if any, sprouted in a vacuum. What are the influencers that make you authentic? Our early life circumstances certainly shape us all. The unique elements that foster an honest and sincere *Authenticity* seem to arise from some kind of moral seedbed as if sprouting from your parents' example, religious influences, social convention, or your own sense of right and wrong.

When we look at the failures of leaders to engage respectfully with their followers, we detect a crack that we must assume has its origins along an inner fault-line, some flaw in their formative authorship. By contrast, the most beloved and inspiring self-authored leaders are those who live a life of moral steadiness. It's as though the leaders we admire are made of something durable enough to withstand the lures of power and prestige. What's the structure of your moral fiber?

Values

As an emerging leader, you realize that you already possess some inner guiding principles. You've been using these beliefs to guide you in decision-making, action, and leading. These personally held principles mesh with society's expectations and form the common human practices that will eventually define the kind of relationships you'll have with others.

Yet here's the problem: as Clare Graves says, "The error which most people make when they think about human values is that they assume the nature of man is fixed and there is a single set of human values by which he should live."[3]

Graves researched and developed a theory of values. He concluded, "That man's nature is an open constantly evolving system, a system which proceeds by quantum jumps from one steady state system to the next through a hierarchy of ordered systems."[4]

Your life's circumstances and especially the social milieu in which you move shape the development of your *Values*. Or as Graves says, "The psychology of the mature human being is an unfolding, emergent, oscillating, spiraling process marked by progressive subordination of older, lower-order behavior systems to newer, higher-order systems as man's existential problems change."[5]

While developing the capacity of *Integrity*, you shape and define your inner compass—your *Values*. The unique type or quality of the *Values* you form will determine the manner in which you deal with threats and opportunities, as well as the nature of your relationships. And most critically, the level of *Values* you develop, compared to the level of *Values* developed by the people you lead, is what will define your ability to engage effectively with other people. For example, if you are holding and acting out of ego-centric *Values*, you will not win the respect of people whose own *Values* are at ethno-centric or world-centric levels, and you're probably not going to survive very long as their leader.

Similarly, your progressive opinions about global markets, product quality, and customer service fall on deaf ears when too many employees do not even receive a living wage. This disparity of *Values* increases as the gulf between the income of the average American worker and that of the average CEO's pay continues to widen.

How do you continue to develop as an Inside*OUT* leader while these inner stirrings of your conscience awaken and urge you to even more courageous moves?

Character

As in the other leadership capacities, it's at this mid-point of capacity development where you evolve in your *Integrity* from an inner experience to an exterior expression. Your inner experience of *Authenticity* and of *Values* is beginning to show up in observable behaviors. *Character* is the occurrence of values-expressed-as-behaviors. It's your *Character* that others are describing when they use words like "consistent" or "walks-the-talk."

Your *Character* is really your capability to be outwardly *Authentic*. With your *Character* on display, others will either applaud your *Integrity* or begin to doubt your relevance to them. As a maturing leader, you also realize that you're responsible for shaping the organization's values as an extension of your own *Character*.

One of the places where a leader's *Character* is most on display is in the area of compensation: payment to self and to others. I recently learned about a young entrepreneur who has several employees among his staff who actually receive greater compensation than he does. And he said that the differential is essential and right, because of the value that these higher-paid-individuals bring to the job. His choice speaks to his *Values*-based *Character*.

I want to shine the spotlight on this compensation issue a bit more because leaders are the ones who are best positioned to make these systemic changes. Perhaps, by following the money, we can also understand the increasing numbers of corrupt leaders. A scathing report by organizational psychologist Tomas Chamorro-Premuzic outlines several metrics of some leaders' greed, and we can infer the probable cost to their organizations.

"CEO compensation has risen by 725% in the past three decades—that's 127 times more than worker pay. In 1978, the average CEO earned 26 times more than the average worker—it's now 210 times more. CEOs of S&P index companies make 354 times more than the average employee."[6]

If you're one of these CEOs referenced by Tomas, would you please explain to the rest of us your rationale for demanding, negotiating, or accepting such high pay ratios for yourself? And if you're an aspiring CEO, here is where you get to assess your own *Values*. Are you calculating your worth in your organization by your *Values*, and therefore your *Character*, or simply by your appetite?

Pay gap disparity is one of the many markers of social inequity that we tolerate in the United States. I've noticed that front-line managers and career advancing leaders seem eager to add increasingly important titles to their positions and the accompanying pay increases. However, I have yet to hear of any who refuse a promotion to ascend the corporate ladder until there is equal pay for women or a reduction in the pay gap between a typical employee and the CEO.

This disparity just might be one of the current versions of previously accepted societal behaviors such as child labor, indentured servitude, or slavery. In 2013, a website called Nerd Wallet shared the results of a study showing that a typical fast food and retail worker at both McDonalds and at Starbucks works more than *six months* to equal *one hour* of compensation of their CEOs.[7] This certainly illustrates the corporate values and social character at play in these and too many other U.S. companies. While it's necessary that Congress and each state pass laws that increases the minimum wage to humane and livable levels, our national character will never become trustworthy unless and until the top end of compensation is also fairly addressed.

Furthermore, this specific aspect of *Character* will not be reconciled as long as so many Americans remain ignorant of these facts. A 2014 journal article cited a study conducted through Harvard Business School that found how uninformed Americans really are. "In the United States...the actual pay ratio of CEOs to unskilled workers (354:1) far exceeded [what Americans estimated the ratio to be] (30:1), which in turn far exceeded the ideal ratio (7:1)"[8]

I see only three possible ways this inequity will be remedied: Workers revolt, government dictates, or leaders actually lead in initiating the values of fairness and compassion. I prefer that we do the latter.

I've elaborated on this issue of leader compensation because that it is at the heart of where Inside*OUT* leaders could make significant change in what the collective attitude is toward leaders in high places. Yet this issue of compensation disparity—and its effects throughout our society—remains a shrill reminder that the emperor has no clothes.

Even though there are many examples of how the undesirable character of some leaders is on display, there is another side to leader *Character*. That is to acknowledge the many leaders who are already guiding their organizations in ways that live out their highest values of caring compassionately for people and planet.

As we discussed earlier, many organizations include social responsibility in their philosophy, literature, operating budgets, and outreach. And these programs are extremely valuable to the communities and entities receiving the attention. We must remember that these nobler efforts are also ways by which an organization's character and its leaders' character are on display.

Some companies, as well as some leaders, practice generous acts of philanthropy. While this before-tax practice is one to gratefully acknowledge, unless economic fairness and justice is dealt with on the front-end of the business, we suspect the real motivation for apparent generosity.

On a much smaller scale than CEO compensation, I've noticed another way that the *Character* of some leaders shows up. Having spent many days working inside many different corporate headquarters and manufacturing centers and having dined with executives and their employees in their cafeterias, those executives who join their employees for lunch always impress me. These companies also seem to convey a convivial spirit among staff as they move from meeting to meeting or as workers go about their duties.

Oh yes, I've also seen (from the outside) a few private executive dining rooms. The employees simply shrugged off those ostentatious displays in the same way a parent might imply, "kids will be kids" and then roll their eyes and return to their usual lunchtime conversation.

How does your *Character* show up within your organization? Is your workplace really a center of community as well as being a hive of productivity? If you are not one of the higher paid employees, would you want to invest 40+ hours every week working in this environment? What is the *Character* of your organization? And what are you consciously doing to make it more of a place where each employee finds relational *and* economic fulfillment?

Ethics

Ethics are the agreed upon behaviors and principles by which a society or an organization governs the individual actions of its members. If you, as the leader, adopt a "code of ethics" and announce it to others, you are saying that you are allowing others to hold you and your behavior accountable; you're committing to the social vitality of your organization.

You're forging relational, organizational, economic, and professional bonds, and these connections are upheld by the mutual adherence of others to these standards. The shared nature of a group's ethics is the baseline from which you promote and follow the principle of "being each other's keeper." Principles like this exist so you can insure the moral development of your peers, your organization, and its people.

However, there's a way that we are all subject to an ongoing erosion of our societal ethics. It has to do with our collective morals and what has happened in this country over the past thirty or more years. Young people in the U.S. under the age of thirty have never lived during a time when our country was not at war. And those of us over fifty can still recall the social tremors that accompanied the Viet Nam War and its fallout.

Consider this. As more and more organizational leaders come from the ranks of America's military forces, we can't help but examine how the United States' collective fascination with a strong military is shaping our societal sense of right and wrong.

We have all heard about PTSD, severe head injuries, and other traumatic injuries. And many of us are living with their effects in our communities. Perhaps you, or someone you know, carry the burden of these disturbing experiences.

Without diminishing the physical, mental, and emotional prices paid by the men and women in uniform, and by their families, there is another condition that none of us escape— *moral injury*. Scientists are paying attention to this sinister, yet widespread, condition. Brett Litz, Professor of Psychiatry at Boston University School of Medicine, and his colleagues define moral injury as, "Perpetrating, failing to prevent, bearing witness to, or learning about acts that transgress deeply held moral beliefs and expectations."[9]

Pulitzer Prize-winning journalist David Wood refers to this injury as the 'signature wound' of today's veterans and as the pain that results from damage to a person's moral foundation.[10] If we use the above definition for moral injury, then I cannot imagine anyone, military or civilian, who is not included in this description? Reread the definition above that Litz and his colleagues use.

Why would I mention moral injury while discussing leadership *Ethics*? Because we are all impacted. There are many returning military personnel working in corporate leadership positions and thus impacting the company's culture. In addition, we civilians have also been impacted, though very differently, by the actions of our military throughout the world.

More broadly, each of us has "learned about acts that transgress deeply held moral beliefs and expectations." In our communities, these acts are not only perpetrated by criminals but also, more appallingly, by those sworn to protect us all. And we continue to learn more about these acts nearly every day. Certainly, we are all affected by these offenses to our moral beliefs and expectations.

Furthermore, without taking away any of the severity and complexity of those with the military experiences mentioned above, the prevalence and visibility of civilian leader wrongdoings cast us all into a kind of moral and ethical quagmire from which we must extricate our organizations and ourselves. We see these violations among people in religious and political positions, as well as in education, law enforcement, and business. There is no sector of society that is immune from these ethical wrongdoings. We are all exposed to moral injury.

It is no wonder then that cynicism and lack of engagement are so widespread in our society, particularly amongst our young people. Many resources cite a lowering of voter turnout, especially young and new voters. Daily or more frequently, if you are on Twitter, you see announcements of yet more outrageous acts by governmental or corporate leaders that defy our social mores and good sense. Generation X'ers are thumbing their collective noses at the noise coming from both sides of the political spectrum and are countering with their own responses—socially liberal yet fiscally conservative.

What does this have to do with this stage of your developing *Ethics*? Many researchers are pointing to the huge shift in the way younger adults are living out their values. Young leaders are bringing a new perspective to how our society must progress and transform. Though this societal tremor happens with each generation, it has been over 50 years since the last major shakeup occurred. And we are now squarely in the active middle of another seismic shift.

What can we do about this? As a leader, consider that people tend to faithfully follow those leaders who adhere to the ethics and morals of their tribe and more importantly to what is honest, true, and just. We want to rub up against that which we want in ourselves. And when we look to our leaders for exemplary behavior, we also expect, no we must demand, them to engage in their own moral *and* professional development. In addition, we expect them to create organizations based on moral excellence. Leaders who are mature in their own capacity of *Integrity* create societies that in return expect their leaders to foster ethical standards— ones by which we become and remain civilized.

Civility

Civility is the collective behaviors and attitudes that embody the highest regard for others within a society. When you, as a leader, guide your organization into this quality of interaction among its personnel and with its public, the foundation is laid for social designs that can unleash the individual and collective spirit.

This stage of development is more than mere courtesy or strict adherence to laws; it includes the highest regard for the authentic self in every individual. It is what philosopher Martin Buber described as the "I/Thou" experience, when the authentic leader fully and genuinely engages with the core sense of self in others. In fact, it is what the "we" experience is really composed of—a sacred union of separate beings that becomes more than the sum of the individual parts.

Genuine interactions assure that the actual intent of commerce is fulfilled—that we use the exchange of goods and services as a way to be in relationship with others and thereby sustain our communities and ourselves. This is the work of civilization. At least, it's the ideal to which we aspire. Except, we aren't there yet.

In a recent study by researchers Rijsenbilt and Commandeur, they explained their results this way.

We…assessed the narcissism levels of 953 CEOs from a wide range of industries, as well as examining objective performance indicators of their companies during their tenure. Unsurprisingly, organizations led by arrogant, self-centered, and entitled CEOs tended to perform worse, and their CEOs were significantly more likely to be convicted for corporate fraud… Interestingly, the detrimental effects of narcissism appear to be exacerbated when CEOs are charismatic, which is consistent with the idea that charisma is toxic because it increases employees' blind trust and irrational confidence in the leader. If you hire a charismatic leader, be prepared to put up with a narcissist.[11]

Instinctively, we know that arrogant self-centered leaders affect more than just their immediate circles. We know that all of us are touched somehow by their behavior. But how?

Use your own experience to validate this. Think back to when you reacted to a leader's questionable behavior. For me,

I recall President Clinton's pathetic explanations about his "inappropriate relationship" with Monica Lewinsky. Though I had voted for him, upon this disclosure I certainly lost confidence in his integrity.

Or how about the leaders in the banking and regulatory institutions in 2007? If one ever doubted the effect that the greed of a relatively few individuals could have, then the recession of 2008 showed us how dependent we all are on the systems created to insure our collective economic safety and the men and women who regulate these systems.

Those in Washington who have been sworn to serve and protect the interests of their constituents and then appear to make decisions based on the security of their own next election serve to embitter so many citizens. It will take noble efforts from future leaders to correct the impact on our democratic processes from the actions of elected officials in both congressional and executive branches of our government.

I'm proposing *Civility* as the epitome of a leaders' capacity for *Integrity,* though it is merely the starting point for a civil society. The Institute for Civility in Government claims.

> Civility is about more than just politeness, although politeness is a necessary first step. It is about disagreeing without disrespect, seeking common ground as a starting point for dialogue about differences, listening past one's preconceptions, and teaching others to do the same.

> Civility is the hard work of staying present even with those with whom we have deep-rooted and fierce disagreements. It is political in the sense that it is a necessary prerequisite for civic action. But it is political, too, in the sense that it is about negotiating interpersonal power such that everyone's voice is heard, and nobody's is ignored.[12]

Yet so many organizations and corporations suffer from the uncivil actions of their leaders. A study by management professors Porath and Pearson outlines four key costs associated with leaders' rudeness: "creativity suffers, performance and team spirit deteriorate, customers turn away, and managing incidents is expensive."[13]

Subsequently, what is your *Capacity for Transparency*? If we examined a "core sample" of you, would we find that you are true all the way through? Can you firmly state your *Values* and their foundations? Are you authoring your own life or are you flowing with the breezes of circumstance and opportunity?

Lastly, do others consider you a person of exemplary *Character* who demonstrates high ethical standards and holds others to the same morals? And are you actively modeling *Civility* and promoting it in your organization?

If you answered anything less than affirmative to the above questions, what then are you going to do to expand *Integrity* through *Authenticity, Values, Character, Ethics and Civility*, and when will you begin?

Coda

What happened with Peter and Apex? Peter began his cleanup at home. He faced his own behavior first and accepted the corrective feedback from his immediate family about the costs to others when he loses his cool. Then he had a meeting with his dad.

Luckily for both Peter and his dad, Frank must have been in a conciliatory mood because he listened carefully and somewhat openly to Peter as he described the stories about Frank's tantrums. Peter told his dad that he was initiating a company-wide zero tolerance policy against bullying and rude behavior.

Peter then worked with several consultants to design the policy, to recruit internal allies, and to plan for how it would be communicated to all the staff. He acknowledged his own imperfect past behavior, and he became the voice in his organization for being real, not pretentious.

He challenged his Board of Directors to adhere to their by-laws and to uphold them even though there were buddy networks and monetary pressures that seemed more important. He met with each of the staff and invested significant time and energy to healing those egregiously hurt.

And he made personal trips to all their major clients to remediate the past pains from Apex's institutionalized uncivil behavior. He became a model for integrity in business and in life. Apex is on track toward its most profitable year ever!

Go confidently
in the direction of your
dreams.
Live the life
you have imagined.
—Henry David Thoreau

5

INSPIRATION
Capacity for
Innovation

Maria

She was the Executive Director for a multi-state healthcare organization. I first met her when I spoke at the annual conference for a national healthcare association. She approached me after my presentation to ask if she could contract with me for one-on-one executive coaching. I was a bit surprised by how she asked; her question seemed more like a directive than a professional request for my services. This was to be my first hint that she took the "director" part of her job title very seriously.

I told her that it's my practice to have an initial meeting to determine our mutual fit for a professional relationship. I didn't want to refuse her just yet because there was something fascinating about her that stood out more than her blunt style. I just wasn't sure what it was. Two weeks later, we met for our initial meeting.

It was clear that she was a driven person. She acted as if some inner mechanical force propelled her. Have you ever met someone who is driven but still radiates a kind of warmth about them? Some individuals seem able to exhibit a drive that originates in their heart, arising from their internal enthusiasm. They seem passionate: not Maria. She didn't smile, nor did she exhibit the least bit of warmth.

I speculated that there were very few people she answered to outside of her Board of Directors. I later discovered that her organization was one in which the tail wagged the dog. The Board was the most impotent group I have ever experienced. Thinking back to that time, I'm still relieved that I had only agreed to work with Maria and had not taken on the entire organization as my client.

Her first and most critical concern was directing everyone in her organization to pull in the same direction. She told me that several of the department heads on her team led their teams with little regard for the vital interfaces that are required in a smoothly working organization. In her world, this disconnect not only jeopardized the vital operations of the organization but also endangered the wellbeing of their customers, its patients.

She recited the many ways and times that she failed in her attempts to corral her team of wild horses. She complained that either a hole in the fence, or the moves by a few bullies, or some other distraction always resulted in the organization working more like a stampeding herd rather than a unified force. So my first directive to her was to take her attention off of others and to look instead at what she was doing, or not doing, which promoted chaos instead of unity.

As you might guess, her willingness to turn from looking outward to turning inward wasn't achieved in an instant. It took many weeks and many attempts, but eventually, she began to loosen her calloused grip on her opinions of others and placed herself on the hot seat.

Early in my work with Maria, I asked her to tell me what excited her. When in her life did she feel most alive, or when did her heart skip a beat? She stopped and looked at me as if I had suddenly placed a broom handle into the spokes of her otherwise smoothly rolling bicycle. When she recovered her ability to speak, she waded through excuses for how all consuming her work really was and how it left no energy for any pursuits of the heart. Then, she recalled the time before her current position when she had more available time and energy. She spoke quietly and slowly as she reminisced about how she had enjoyed handcrafts and creating apparel with fabrics. This was the first time I saw an actual person emerge from behind her steely executive facade.

I coached Maria for more than three years, and during that time, she frequently spoke of challenges she was having with one of her senior team members or with her Board of Directors. As she described some of her team members, it was easy for me to see how she had become so absorbed with maintaining some cohesion in the organization. Each of her departmental executives was highly qualified in their own field, but it seemed to me that she had hired and appointed emotionless clones of herself. Consequently, the executive team lacked any sense of warmth.

After working on her *Identity*, she became eager to reclaim her role as maestro of the organization. To do so, she first had to rekindle the fire that brought her to this field of work in the first place. She remembered her early mentors and what had so motivated her to persevere in her career. She described the courageous work of one young woman who had founded an educational and medical program for Central American children living in extreme poverty. Maria was very touched by the commitment and far-sightedness of this young person. Maria had vowed to redirect her early medical career into a leadership role. Now she admitted, after several months of working with me, that she had lost touch with her dreams and with all the activities that brought her joy.

I asked Maria what so captured her about this young woman. She sat for several long seconds in silence, looking out the window with a faraway expression. Finally, she turned to look at me. Her face and voice took on the peculiar combination of both laser-like clarity and profound wistfulness.

She began to speak. "It was her vision. She always seemed able to see something that no one else could see. She spoke often of her dream for those children. Someday, they would be physically nurtured and healthy. They could spend their days in school instead of their years scavenging for food. And yet she simply went about her work with a purpose that drew so many other people to her cause."

Over the next several sessions, while reflecting on the model of this young woman, Maria began to reconnect with the excitement that she had experienced in her own first roles as a leader. She reminisced about seeing the eagerness of her first team members to build a clinic that supported the needs of pregnant women in her city. She must have had an energy pack that was driving her, and I wanted her to tap back into that experience and the many other sources she had once accessed. I wanted her to refuel her spirit. She had clearly lost her way. More importantly, she really wanted to get her mojo back.

Maria was a very driven person, yet somewhere along her career path, she had lost the source of her commitment and was no longer having any fun. Once she reignited her heart from the spark of her values and linked her deep compassion for others with the reason she chose to lead clinicians who cared for the sick and injured, she began to experience an energy that had gone dormant. She had remained driven but not passionate. She performed well in her job, but she was fumbling along without an articulate and motivating picture of how the organization could actually serve. She was leading a team of equally driven people but toward an ill-defined future and without a compelling map. She was without a vision.

Once she arrived at this realization, she was ready to engage with her team in a creative and collaborative way to create the future she could now imagine for their organization. For many coaching sessions, she worked at shaping her unspoken sense of what she really was seeking into a coherent and exciting vision for herself and for her organization. She realized that although she had always sensed where she wanted to go, she hadn't formed those vague impressions into a clear picture. No wonder she was unable to point her team in a unified direction. She couldn't yet describe it to herself.

It was during this time in our work together that she picked up her textile arts once again. I asked her how she knew what to make or what designs she "saw." I was trying to help her link the process of visualization that she already experienced in her creative art projects to the process of visualizing for her organization's future. Many people find it difficult to envision their tomorrows or to describe to others the images in their heads. As a leader, you must be able to both imagine and to articulate to others what you see. If you cannot use your own words to describe where you're going and where you want to take the organization, others can't follow you and will merely wander in their own directions.

During one of our sessions, Maria was eager to tell me about the gifts she was making for her two grown sons. Her dad had died the year before, and as a way to keep his memory alive for herself and for her sons, she imagined a way that they could always remember their grandfather. While sorting through her father's belongings, she had noticed all his shirts that were still hanging in his closet. Something clicked for her. Her dad had been a professional man but did not need to wear a white shirt and tie every day. Instead, he had a huge supply of well-made tailored shirts in conservative stripes, checks, and plaids.

She took this huge pile of shirts and began to cut squares from the fabric. She eventually pieced together hundreds of small squares into two quilted throws. She gave one to each of her sons. When she showed me pictures of her project, the first thing I noticed was the straight-line shapes of the plaids and stripes that represented her dad. There was not a single solid, paisley, swirl, or Hawaiian floral.

She was then able to translate her artistic processes into her professional endeavor, and within a few weeks, she showed me the draft of notes for the upcoming executive team's annual meeting. She had painted a compelling picture of where she planned to take the organization in the next three years. I can still recall the light on her face when she read her notes to me. Her previously metallically severe face now radiated a glow as if fueled by some inner warmth. I now saw the evidence for that fascinating something I had first seen in her when we met nearly a year before at the medical association conference.

Maria polished her appeal to the annual organizational meeting, and she delivered it. Her team members also noticed the difference in their leader, and several responded favorably to her challenge. A remaining few crossed their arms defiantly. Later as she told me about the meeting, she laughed softly about how she saw her previous self in those worried team members, and she declared to win them over within six months.

I was so lucky to have had a front row seat during that time. She was trying out new ways to lead. She experimented with this newly recovered desire to support people toward health. Those providing services to the sick and injured especially moved her. She promoted ideas for how her team and how her organization could contribute in their communities in a much more concerted manner. Maria was now leading her team from the power of her passion and her drive to serve. She had inspired her team to join her, and they embraced her vision as their own.

Inspiration—Capacity for Innovation

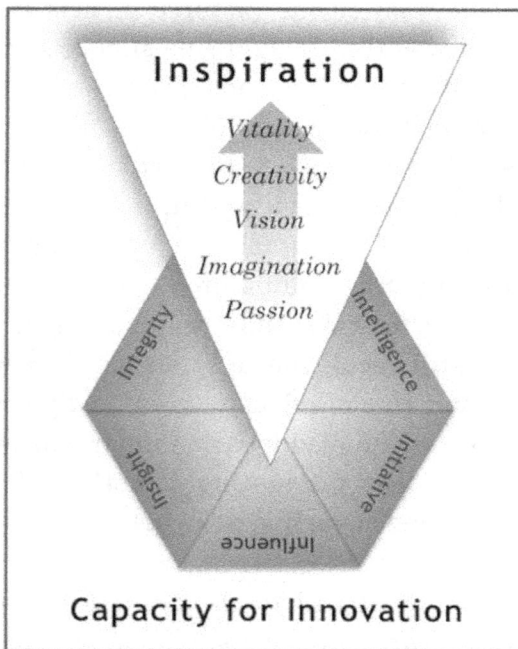

Inspiration is the capacity that enables you to see the possible. It springs from the energy of the heart, from boundless ingenuity, and from innovation that propels us beyond the known and into the pristine realm of originality. This *Capacity for Innovation* invites you to have experiences that are beyond the ordinary. *Inspiration* infuses and activates your heart and your mind. And it even energizes your body. Look at all those runners at your local 10K, half-marathon, or Ironman races. Most of these part-time athletes would point to someone or something that inspired them. And haven't you been roused in your spirit at least once in your life while viewing a sunset, while listening to a piece of music, or when witnessing another person overcome insurmountable odds?

Nevertheless, there's a wrinkle in these memories of feel-good times. Most people who speak about *Inspiration* only know the experience of being inspired because someone else has acted in a way that touched or moved them, not because they were the source of another's *Inspiration*. Perhaps most of us are just too modest to claim that we inspire others, but my question is just between you and me. Can you point to a way or a time that you lifted another's spirit so that they went on to act in ways they never would have thought possible? Are there individuals out there who would list your name among their champions, among those who inspired them?

To be able to be inspired is essential for this capacity, but it is not sufficient. *Inspiration*, like breathing, is something to be taken in, but it is not complete unless it is also expressed outwardly. *Inspiration* definitely includes this receptive aspect, except it's only fully developed when you, as a leader, are also a source of energy, stimulation, and deep stirrings for others. Others are the ones who get to vote when, or not, you've developed your capacity of *Inspiration*.

Lance Secretan, leadership mentor and CEO of Manpower Limited, describes the unique nature of inspiration this way.

Motivation, which is based on fear, comes from the personality. Inspiration, which is based on love, comes from the soul...What if we could inspire others by appealing to something within them that is far greater than the personality or the ego? What if we could excite something emotional or intuitive that is at the very essence of our humanness? What would we call this if we could find it, work with it, and engage it? I think we would call this ineffable thing the *soul*—the holiness and sacredness within us that is larger than anything we can imagine in the narrow definition of personality or ego— something that is the mystical, magical, and extraordinary essence that is the life force in each of us.[1]

Remember the deck prism in the old sailing ship and how the energy of the light is magnified as it passes through the prism? So too, *Inspiration* is energy, and to be effective, it must pass through you, not just stop with you being touched. Leading implies that all those in your circle, family, friends, and followers, will be moved by the energy that radiates through you.

I have been touched and moved by many individuals. And I thoroughly enjoy learning about the innovative efforts of others. I love the boost, the lift, and the heart tugs that come with learning about individuals who have gone way beyond the ordinary. I guess it's a vicarious high for me; I get to feel some of the gain with none of their pain.

When my youngest son was in high school, I had to examine my desire to be inspired while not becoming the source of energy for others. The school my son attended focused on not only helping young people discover their unique potential but included the student's entire family in activities designed to create a healthy household. One of the first parent assignments we received in our curriculum invited us to look at one of our key responsibilities: to inspire our children.

Sounds pretty simple, right? I'll just tell him how far I had to walk to school when I was a kid, and that I had to carry my packed lunches, and that I felt inferior because I was skinny. This will really inspire him to appreciate how much better his life is than mine was. Essentially, I'll tell him how grateful he should be. What's so hard about that? I tell him what to do and how to behave all the time.

I was way off base. Then I paid attention to exactly how we parents might, I repeat might, inspire our youth. The directions were simple but really difficult to execute. I was to take a walk with my teenager and on the walk to not ask anything about him. I was to simply, and candidly, talk about a struggle that I was currently having in my life, not about something that occurred in the past. I was to detail my challenge with special attention on how I was feeling. I recall using words like scared and embarrassed. For me, that walk along the beach was a powerful turning point in my relationship with my son. I let go of my perceived job to fix everything for him, and I simply joined him as another human struggling through life.

The point of the exercise was to reveal to our kids that we don't have all the answers; we're really not as well put together as we might appear to be. Young people simply need to know that they are not the only ones in the family with challenges. Clearly, that experience affected me deeply and has stayed with me for nearly twenty years.

I don't believe those who actually inspire others set out by trying to impress them. They are simply going about their own lives, facing their struggles, figuring it out, or not, and humbly doing what needs to be done. They are honest and open about their own struggles with their family or teams. And through the experience with my son, I learned what it meant to actually inspire another.

The writer, David Foster Wallace, had a sense of what it meant to inspire when he wrote, "Real leaders are people who help us overcome the limitations of our own laziness and selfishness and weakness and fear and get us to do better, harder things than we can get ourselves to do on our own."[2]

Yet as leaders, and as parents, we tend to resort to a typical method of pushing others to go in the direction we think they should go. We get behind them and shove. We fail to get out in front and let our own sweat and stumbles become their map. We must become much more skillful at distinguishing between propulsion and magnetism.

Inspiration, like each of the other capacities for leading, expands not by focusing on being inspiring, but as a result of your careful cultivation of several other traits. When many of us think about *Inspiration,* we immediately associate it with charisma. If someone told you to be more inspiring, you probably wouldn't know exactly what to do. You'd be thinking: should I smile more, should I be perkier around the office, or should I be more generous and light-hearted with my compliments? Is that how to be charismatic? Well, not exactly.

When you attempt any of these behaviors, it simply comes off to others as insincere, like you're acting rather than simply being yourself. Intentional enthusiasm is a dead giveaway and certainly not inspiring. In fact, you will likely suffer the opposite result of being inspiring; you could be perceived as insincere or creepy.

As you nurture your other leadership capacities through the stages I discuss in this material, you'll also, and simultaneously, be expanding your capacity of *Inspiration*. This is the "rising tide lifts all boats" effect that you read about back in chapter one. And here's how it happens.

The stages of *Inspiration* are first experienced internally as the spark of *Passion*. Then it ignites into a flame of possibility through your *Imagination*. As an Inside*OUT* leader, you will then translate those inner stirrings into a lucid *Vision*, something you have imagined and that now you must articulate. As your capacity expands and you're forming what you envisioned, you'll engage in *Creativity*. And then, as at the fifth stage of all the capacities, you'll enter into a perpetual flow of *Vitality,* the source of energy for your enterprise. Let's start near your center, at *Passion*.

Passion

We all love that feeling of being inspired, that upwelling blend of admiration for another person and for what they have achieved. You might also experience a similar feeling through your own actions when you sense the possibility that you might even exceed your own limits. Whether you're aroused by a stirring passage of music, a child's first piano recital, a moving portrayal by an actor, the incredible stamina of an athlete who uses adaptive equipment to be able to engage in a sport, or the loyalty of a colleague when you're challenged by your peers, we all feel a special something in a very deep place.

Inspiration, at this stage, is all about the heart. We feel these inner stirrings as emerging waves, arising from engaging with something outside of ourselves. We're calling this sensation, *Passion*. Yes, the feelings are very similar to the way we feel when we fall feverishly in love.

Except, for our purposes here, I'm using *Passion* to mean the energy that arises from within and fires your enthusiasm for some*thing*, not some*one*. It may be experienced as an emotional boost or perhaps as a force borne of jubilant obligation and duty. *Passion* is most fully experienced as a desire that pulls us toward a giving of our selves in service to an external cause that is larger than we are. Leaders with *Passion* indicate that they are fully activated by something deeply mysterious. They have been touched, moved, and inspired. Yes, they have been stirred, but are they also able to stir, to embolden, and cause another to go beyond their own preconceived constraints?

The measure of many leaders is their ability to inspire. Then how does a leader develop it in the first place? A leader who inspires must first be able to be inspired. What is it that can so possess you that you would use the word "passionate" to describe another? Do you have a soft spot that can be warmed? If you aren't certain about your own *Passion* quotient then perhaps you are a bit leery to let your heart become excited.

On the other hand, if you intend to undertake the work required of expanding this capacity, you'll need to exercise your heart by welcoming in a variety of sources such as beauty, nature, music, art, outstanding acts, or literature. Or you might choose to learn about other men and women who test their own mettle and contribute to our collective understanding of human endurance. Or you might set out to surpass your own previously perceived limits as a way to stimulate your spirit.

Regardless of the way you choose to kindle your spark, you will certainly stir your soul as well. Being just out of reach is a common characteristic of something that inspires. You recognize that you must stretch yourself in some extraordinary way if you are to ignite the spark and to release the energy available to you.

Best selling author Daniel Coyle wrote about rocker Keith Richard's passion for music and how he fell in love with the guitar.

> Keith's Grandpa Gus, who was a former musician and a bit of a rebel, noticed that Keith liked singing... Whenever young Keith would come over, Gus placed a guitar on top of the family piano. Keith noticed. Gus told him, when he was taller, he could give it a try... One momentous and unforgettable day, Gus took the guitar down from the piano, and handed it to Keith. From that moment, Richards was hooked (his first addiction). He took the guitar everywhere he went.[3]

This example of how *Passion* is generated is instructive in several ways. I imagine that Grandpa Gus was engaging, not detached. And there were several things he did that were designed to have specific effects on young Keith.

First, he was aware both of his grandson and of the instruments he had in his house. He observed. Most of us have no time for this step. We want to create instant gratification. But Gus could see the future.

Second, Gus generated a thirst in young Keith. He articulated a vision for Keith's future; he told him that when he became taller he could try it out.

Third, when the time came, he remembered to make a specific connection between Keith and the guitar.

At least this is how I interpret the way Gus ignited the spark of *Passion* in his grandson. It's great when a mentor, or wise teacher, or a family member can guide us, but what about now? What about your life today? How can you engender your own *Passion*?

It requires deliberate awareness. It's not random; it doesn't just happen to you. You must cause it to occur. Then you need to imagine, grasp, and define a *Vision* of the future. Eventually, you realize your intention; you complete the journey.

Listening to how others describe their work shows the degree of *Passion* that they possess. And *Passion* is infectious. One immediately feels that stirring in the heart. I especially enjoy the boost I feel when I watch the TED videos of Benjamin Zander, conductor of the Boston Philharmonic Orchestra. He introduces an audience to the powerful messages in classical music, and his exuberance flows naturally from his joyful spirit. It's impossible to not be touched by him in turn.

But you might be countering, Zander is in the arts, and people like him are used to performing. It's their profession. It's easier for them to be passionate.

I agree that performers can appear a certain way regardless of how they actually feel at the moment. Essentially, their profession expects them to bring forth a feeling to ignite their actions. This is the hardest aspect of performing. If they fail, you don't want to see them again. Except, I do not agree that it is easier for them to be passionate than those in other lines of work.

Who are the types of people who we stereotypically think of as not passionate but blasé, or perhaps even apathetic? Who are those that run cool instead of warm or even hot? In our culture, we often see statisticians and tech types portrayed as people who are pretty calm, perhaps even appearing indifferent. Yet there are many examples of individuals who don't fit that bias. Yes, with some of these people, we need to listen more carefully or look a bit deeper to detect their spark of *Passion*, but it is still there. Just because someone's social traits are more introverted and their profession is more analytical does not mean they are dull. Take a moment to watch the late Hans Rosling in his presentations from the TED stage. He was a professor, statistician, and analyst. Boring? Not a chance.

Regardless of whether you experience someone else's enthusiasm or you feel your own overflowing exuberance, you are touched in a deep place, that precious place in your heart and in the heart of every human. If for no other reason than this, you must become a sentinel for the human spirit by constantly promoting and protecting the dwelling place of *Passion* within yourself and within those who follow you.

Poet and philosopher David Whyte has unpacked this deep soulful experience of *Passion* in a way to which each of us can relate.

To some extent, while we think we are simply driving to work every morning to earn a living, the soul knows it is secretly engaged in a life-or-death struggle for its existence. As a nation we have chosen to invest enormous amounts of our time and energy in the corporate American workplace, so much time and energy, in fact, that the soul is often forced to choose our work environment, even if it is measured by the short length of a desk, as the place it will make or break its way to the surface for existence or 'die' in the attempt. No matter how confined, to the soul everything is at stake, and everything in the flame of that existence is to be lost or won.[4]

When I think of *Passion*, I almost always see my friend, Dirk. I learned to really appreciate him when we served on the executive committee of a Board of Trustees; he was the Treasurer. And that seemed like a great role for him since he was a Harvard educated economist. For several years, we both had offices in the same building, and occasionally, we would wander into the other's office for a chat, some needed office supplies, or a cup of coffee.

Dirk went on to become a state senator for several terms and then was a key sponsor of the ranked choice voting initiative in our state. His unbridled joy infects everyone who knows him, especially when he talks about his work. In fact, when he talks, he makes the convoluted machinations of economics and politics sound humorously delightful. It's simply because he expresses his *Passion* out loud.

Even though few of us actually show our *Passion*, you should start with the question: do you experience *Passion* for anything? What so captures your heart that you forget to eat, you stay up all night, and you can think about little else? The bottom line is, what touches, moves, and inspires you? Is it your partner, your children, your teammates, or a sunrise?

Go ahead, show your excitement for what you achieved or how your team overcame the obstacles and shipped the product on time. Smile, laugh, play and engage in an activity that makes you say, wow, as if you tasted joy for the first time.

If you ever hope to inspire others, you will need to become passionate about something. The process of becoming a leader who inspires others begins with having *Passion* stirring in your own heart. Without it, there is little expectation that you will be able to touch, move, or inspire anyone. And remember, as a leader, you're success is dependent upon influencing others.

Inspiration flows from an aroused heart and quickly envelops the rest of your being, especially your mind. Now let's look at how *Passion* moves from your heart to your mind as it becomes *Imagination.*

Imagination

Imagination is your capability to engage your mind in a process that moves a vague notion or impulse into a clearer picture. This ability implies that you are affected by something usually outside of yourself. Then your mind makes meaning out of the stimulus. To develop *Imagination,* you must spend some conscious time exploring circumstances that require new solutions rather than accepting what is easy or yielding to an unconscious immersion into day-to-day tasks.

Repeatedly employing resourcefulness when faced with challenges, curiosity, or opportunity will flex your mental muscles, and eventually *Imagination* will become a familiar occurrence. And as you stimulate your mind with attention on potential pathways through the unknown, you will gain ease and artistry with problem solving. That will lead you to the next stages in this capacity.

In his book *The Innovators*, Walter Isaacson wrote about the intersection of *Passion* and *Imagination*, of heart and head. He wrote, "Like many aspects of the digital age, this idea that innovation resides where art and science connect is not new. Leonardo da Vinci was the exemplar of the creativity that flourishes when the humanities and sciences interact. When Einstein was stymied while working out General Relativity, he would pull out his violin and play Mozart until he could reconnect to what he called the harmony of the spheres."[5]

Regrettably, when a leader is elected, appointed, or hired, their passion and imagination are seldom taken into consideration. In some cases, a candidate's record of innovation might be considered, but usually the hiring decision makers focus on the candidate's subject matter expertise, technical skill, past performance, steadiness, directness, or other attributes that imply strength. A candidate's artistic or creative competency is rarely considered since these traits seem to be foreign notions for many leadership positions.

However, I assert that leaders must possess a significant *Capacity for Innovation* if they are to be taken seriously. Those of us with aging lines recall that rousing display of *Imagination* in 1961 when President Kennedy announced to a joint session of Congress that the United States would land a man on the moon and return him safely to earth before the end of the decade. That outlandish declaration required an incredible *Imagination*. At that time, the U.S. didn't have the science, budget, or mental context for such an audacious claim. And since the Soviets led the U.S. in space accomplishments, competition was keen. Any idea that placed America ahead of the Soviet Union quickly galvanized the necessary support for JFK's challenge.

JFK's speech has become a model for *Inspiration*. This speech illustrates the power of *Imagination*. He was not stating the easy or obvious. At that time, human occupation of another planet or the moon was only stuff of science fiction.

In our society, especially in our business culture, leaders are generally not considered the creative types. Though their instruments may not be paint, pencil, or piano, a leader has, however, a unique yet powerful device that is similarly moldable—the organization. In our society, we grant our leaders tremendous influence over our lives. If you aspire to become an individual who will inspire others to ever-greater feats, you must develop the part of you that is an artist. You must become someone who can imagine something that does not yet exist or is not yet present in your organization.

What would you like to see in your organization? What needs or desires exist out there that your organization might meet? What products or services can you imagine? What might you fashion from the raw material of your organization? Imagine what or how your organization might be. Is there a different way for personnel to relate within the organization that would be more consistent with your values and with the stated aims and values of your organization?

But before you stand in front of your Board of Directors or the annual meeting of the home office staff to announce your own version of a moon shot, let's return to a more personal level. Let's begin with you. Do you dream? When have you allowed yourself to color outside the lines? What would it take for you to abandon conformity and to simply imagine? What would it be like if you allowed your *Passion* to drive your *Imagination*? What if you began to envision something?

Look around you right now and notice how everything that you can see or experience which is not of nature is the result of someone's imagination. Look up from this page. The door handle, the pen on your desk, the piece of music playing in the background, the musical instruments and each of their little parts, the window frame and its glass, a paper clip; even the pyramids of Giza, Mount Rushmore, jet skis, Habitat for Humanity, and many more examples from the commonplace to the sublime. Just imagine how easy your life is in this moment because you're the beneficiary of the imaginings of thousands of innovators throughout history. A limited *Imagination* stifles so many leaders, and because of that, many people follow them into a future of only partial possibilities. The Inside*OUT* leader gets in front of an idea, a trend, or a curve and then invites, but doesn't compel, others to follow.

Albert Einstein once said, "Imagination is more important than knowledge. For knowledge is limited to all we now know and understand, while imagination embraces the entire world, and all there ever will be to know and understand."[6]

When did you start to place acquisition of knowledge over flights of imagination? What caused many of us to abandon our hours of play with blocks, Hot Wheels, and Barbie dolls? When you watch children at play now, just notice how they can entertain themselves for hours with little more than found objects or no objects at all? Remember that certain age when all the gifts that a child received for a birthday or holiday were less interesting than the boxes in which the presents arrived? A child's brain has so much more capacity for imagination. Why do most of us lose that capability as we age?

Einstein hints at this loss when he mentions knowledge. As we age, we accumulate more information, more knowledge, and in our educational processes, we are pushed to pack on even greater amounts of data. Now you may be an individual who resists info in favor of form or flow. Or perhaps you're one of the few who is drawn to do something others say cannot be done. Neuroscientist Gregory Berns calls this individual an "iconoclast." He tells us that the iconoclast's, "...brain differs in these three functions and the circuits that implement them: Perception, fear response, and social intelligence."[7]

Let's look at you. In your *Capacity for Innovation*, you might be exploring an area that is possibly quite foreign to you. In your role as leader, you're asked to decide, to execute, and to operate within a budget. And you're compensated for how well you do all that. And that allows precious little brain reserves for dreaming, for imagining, or for innovating. What are you able to do in order to expand your ability to imagine?

The first difference in neural wiring that Berns identified has to do with the *visual system* of the iconoclast.

Perhaps it is a result of the way we are educated, or perhaps it is simply a reflection of a biological maturation of our brain, but creativity seems to become more difficult for many people as they get older. The efficiency principle, coupled with the consolidation of large amounts of information and experience as we get older, means that the brain needs to categorize. And yet, imagination stems from the ability to break this categorization, to see things not for what one thinks they are, but for what they might be.[8]

Our brains automatically categorize information in order to make life easier and to make room for more information. Because this action of our brain is automatic, we need to stretch our periphery, our fields of interests, and we need to go where we've never been. Berns suggests, "The surest way to evoke the imagination is to confront the perceptual system with people, places, and things it hasn't seen before. Categories are death to imagination. So the solution is to seek out environments in which you have no experience. The environments may have nothing to do with the individual's area of expertise."[9]

My brother is an iconoclast. He is the founder and developer of a unique senior community campus. In order for his dream to become reality, he imagined ways to provide interactions for the residents that he based on the way typical healthy towns and villages actually function. He made sure that the residents would interact with the larger community as well as receive the best personal support possible. He insisted that all services were to be delivered in cost effective ways for the individuals actually receiving the assistance or care. He was not interested in methods designed to make the accountant's job easier or the shareholders wealthier. As a businessperson and social worker, he believes that the whole person and a sensitive community need to relate in mutually dependent and beneficial ways.

It might have been easier, and certainly more routine, to simply outsource the design of those features and systems to a medical professional or to a facilities developer. On the contrary, my brother imagined how he would prefer to age in a community that assisted and supported his aging needs rather than merely cared for them. He believed that older adults should not be treated like patients who need care. They should be regarded as people who could look after themselves so they could retain their autonomy even in some very simple ways. Hence, he created housing, support systems, and processes to fulfill his dream and meet the needs of many delighted seniors.

He pushed against the prevalent medical approach for designing services and structures for seniors. He imagined an entire campus that would provide services within a full range of dwellings from active retirees' privately owned homes to apartments for adults needing individualized assistance and daily activities, to a multi-level health-care facility providing rehabilitation and long-term support for those individuals requiring medical and therapeutic assistance. In addition, he even saw ways that the dwellings could be designed and structured to promote the independence of residents who are facing declining mobility. For example, residents can move about anywhere in the dwellings because there are no steps. And they can move all around the campus without needing steps to accommodate for elevation gain. In order to make his dream a reality, he needed to challenge existing building codes and health care regulators who could not see what he had already envisioned. He prevailed and created a stunning campus. His ability to see things *not for what one thinks they are, but for what they might be* proved to be his most significant achievement.

But admiring an iconoclast's accomplishments is not how you will learn and grow. Your challenge is to expand your own perception by creating the less common solution, by not settling for off-the-shelf answers, and by dreaming how something might be.

Each of us can imagine, even those of us who didn't inherit the iconoclast gene but still want to expand our ability to dream. In the next chapter, you will see how our brains can adjust, how they can shift functions from one circuit to another, and how they can even heal from some injuries. For now though, let's return to the processes that result in *Inspiration*. Let's look at what occurs after your *Passion* lights a spark in your *Imagination*. What might have begun as a mere figment will now erupt into a much clearer idea.

Vision

The firing of your *Imagination*, especially as a result of your aroused *Passion*, nearly always results in the stage of *Vision*. What you "see" in your mind's eye would remain in the realm of your *Imagination* if you don't continue to make your dream real. *Vision* is the intentional process of moving the possible to the actual. It results in some form of manifestation. Articulating a *Vision* requires that you have pondered the language of your own heart. *Imagination* seeks to become conveyed. It wants to see your concept converted into words and deeds that inspire others.

Your imaginings will evaporate if you don't convert them into your *Vision*. It's not enough to have an idea of where you want to go or a future you want to create. You must first marinate your ideas in the juices of your *Passion* and then do something concrete about it. Thomas Edison is reported to have said that vision without execution is hallucination. As someone who imagined and produced over 1,000 items for U.S. patents, he must have some inkling of what's required of you to have a vision.

Throughout my consulting and coaching career, I had the delightful experience of working with leaders and their organizations to define their vision. Those days of having a front row seat at the birthing of individual and collective imagination always made my heart beat just a bit faster. It was exciting to see a leader work with a team through the mental obstacles and the communication barriers to come to the "aha moment" when they could actually see and hear those previously unvoiced dreams and possibilities take shape in a shared space.

One of the hurdles most groups had to overcome was the language they'd use to describe their vision. The teams would often create their first drafts using verbs that pointed to the future. In this way, they were not yet fully imagining their future. Because they used future tense verbs, such as "We will..." their vision remained like an untethered balloon out in front of their grasp, unable to be realized and forever unattainable. If you are to envision a tomorrow that is different from today, you must describe that future state as if it is currently occurring in the present tense.

Occasionally, a leader comes along who deserves the title of visionary. And just to be clear, in case you imagine that title for yourself some day, it will never happen if you are someone who hallucinates or someone who merely dreams and imagines. Those who have imagined a more perfect future, then described to others what they saw as if it already existed, and then rolled up their sleeves and made the *Vision* real are more likely to be the ones we honor.

There is a very brief improvised-in-the-moment ending to a speech that many of us recall when we think about visionary language. Martin Luther King Jr. spoke in 1963 at the March on Washington for Jobs and Freedom about the inequalities so commonplace in American society. Yet as a true visionary, King didn't simply describe the injustices in the existing situation. What he is most remembered for is how eloquently he described a future state, "I have a dream..."

For over four years, he continued to walk boldly into a future he saw and revealed to us. Since he was killed in 1968, it remains his words from that day in 1963 that still capture our collective imagination. Many of us continue to persevere in efforts to defeat racism and to provide opportunities for all.

King's speech is a great example of the power of a *Vision* that is shared. Yet many leaders, especially entrepreneurs, keep their dream in their heads. They guard their *Vision* carefully as if to articulate it would result in giving away their precious ideas. In his book, *Traction*, Gino Wickman aims to provide the incentive and the tools for entrepreneurs to become leaders of their enterprises. He pleads, "Entrepreneurs must get their vision out of their heads and down onto paper. From there, they must share it with their organization so that everyone can see where the company is going and determine if they want to go there [too]."[10]

However, here's the kicker for you as an Inside*OUT* leader. Your *Vision* must be about your greater purpose, your cause, and your gift back to your community. Wickman adds, "The first step is letting go because the vision you're about to clarify can't be about you. It has to define something bigger. You need to create a vision that points the way toward a greater good. The sooner you do that, the sooner you will make better decisions that build an enduring company."[11]

Among all your leadership capacities, it is in your *Capacity for Innovation* that you'll need to act deliberately. You'll need to intentionally let go of something private and offer it up into the public space. Your *Vision* must be shared, and that can be a scary thing to do. You may fear that others will criticize its merits, or weigh its feasibility, or even worse, some might wonder if your brainchild is really yours.

When this fear shows up, you are faced with a choice; a choice that is not necessarily the result of your rational analytical processes. So far, this entire process of *Inspiration* has been held close to your heart, even your soul, and that is why you feel so fervently about your dreams. When you speak with conviction from that very deep place within you, just as Martin Luther King Jr. did, you can activate many other bodily systems that may experience fear yet not be afraid.

This seems paradoxical, but you can give human evolution credit for equipping you with systems that can read a situation as a threat and simultaneously act, in spite of the consequences, by weighing your passion-driven tenacity against danger or a perceived risk. This is why some people can enter burning buildings to rescue a child, or lift a crushing weight off of an injured person, or stand up to hateful taunts, or run a 100-mile race, or speak to the annual meeting of the Board, or even reveal their dream for their organization.

You may face many occasions that will test your resolve. And when they occur, even if your mouth gets dry and your knees feel weak, you might have one more card to play. As we've already seen in past chapters and will find in the remaining ones, when you expand your leadership capacities, you will have developed powerful connections with other people. This ability to connect with others is a necessary asset in your social accounting. You still want to be a leader, don't you? Gregory Berns writes, "Two aspects of social intelligence figure prominently in success or failure: familiarity and reputation. The two go hand in hand. In order to sell one's ideas, one must create a positive reputation that will draw people toward something that is initially unfamiliar and potentially scary. Familiarity helps build one's reputation."[12]

He further explains how networking with others and disclosure of your dream to others builds familiarity. Others need to hear about your *Vision,* but they must also experience you as reliable and trustworthy. The strength of your connections is based on how you behave. These two interdependent factors of familiarity and reputation are vital to communicating your picture of the future. You must find ways for others, lots of others, to hear about your idea, *and* you must exercise your *Integrity* so that others will trust you and your dream.

Yet not all dreams and visions are equal. Some are merely a leader's hallucinations of grandeur. Using too many superlatives like fantastic, terrific, and special to describe your own ideas implies insecurity on your part as well as the fragility of your proposal. Simply share your visions, and if they're praiseworthy, others will supply the superlatives. They will get onboard with your dream because it releases energy among your followers. It's like a fire that is fanned by the wind, captivating the attention of anyone within its area of influence.

Peter Senge and colleagues remind us that some "...ideas unleash no energy for change while others transform the world. 'There is nothing more powerful than an idea whose time has come,' said Victor Hugo one hundred and fifty years ago. Yet, the power Hugo refers to remains elusive, carefully guarded by a paradox: there's nothing more personal than vision, yet the visions that ultimately prove transformative have nothing to do with us as individuals."[13]

Back in the 1990's, I was searching for a way to describe what I sensed was happening and what could happen within the organizations I studied. There seemed to be some force or energy that infused these social institutions with life. I believed that it was something more than simply the combined and faithful efforts of the people involved in executing the organizations' missions and policies. What animated these entities? I couldn't label what I sensed back then, but I recall believing that the forces and energies were not based on linear cause and effect or on projections from last quarter's balance sheet. I believed that there was more than the sum of the organizational structures, departments, roles, and initiatives. Something else was going on that I couldn't describe as input, throughput, or output. I was trying to understand the whole by looking at the parts.

That was when I discovered Margaret Wheatley's writings. She interpreted the elements of quantum physics applying them to the world of organizations and leadership. She gave us some effective language that helped me explain what I believe happens in an organization. She begins by describing how we've assigned concepts for the way our organizations are formed and how they operate based on the mechanical principles formulated during the Newtonian era.

You're probably wondering how we got from discussing *Vision* to quantum theory. I'll explain. Since our collective imagination, science, and experience has evolved quite a bit since Sir Isaac's time, wouldn't it be wise for us to consider upgrading how we think about and create our organizations as well? Along with the sciences, perhaps leadership and organizational dynamics can evolve from images of machines made up of parts to notions of relativity and even to applications of field theory. Perhaps it is our assumptions that need to be updated. Wheatley wrote.

> Field theory can educate us in several ways about how to manage the more amorphous sides of organizations. For example, *vision*—the need for organizational clarity about purpose and direction—is a wonderful candidate for field theory. In linear fashion, we have most often conceived of vision as thinking into the future, creating a *destination* for the organization. We believed that the clearer the image of the destination, the more force the future would exert on the present, pulling us into that desired future state...But what if we changed the science and looked at vision as a field? What if we saw a field of vision that needed to permeate organizational space, rather than viewing vision as a linear destination?[14]

Wow, imagine yourself and your team using that context for crafting your vision statement at an offsite session. You would then need to create a complete ecosystem wherein your vision, and future visions, could dwell. This approach begins to point toward what some theorists call whole companies, holistic organizations, or integral business.

We've already used both artistic and scientific language to describe ways that you might expand your *Capacity for*

Innovation. And the process of expanding this capacity has morphed through the stages of *Passion, Imagination,* and *Vision.* You've revealed your dream to others, and you are now poised on the edge of making what you saw become real. Your idea can now sprout wings.

Creativity

Creativity is the process of transforming an imagined possibility that hasn't existed before into material reality. Of all the capacities, this is the one where you are most likely to experience the mystical. The entire manifest world that is not provided by nature is the result of someone's imagination at work. This process of bringing into material reality something that never existed before requires the utilization and coordination of each of your other capacities.

Like Maria transforming her dad's shirts into cozy blankets for her sons, *Creativity* doesn't arise out of thin air as if by a magician. For her, drinking from her *Imagination* and her *Creativity,* she made something that never existed before. She made blankets out of raw materials that were never considered for this new purpose.

When you move between all that is and all that could be, you are very likely going to have some moments that will unnerve you. Those moments in your life when you're certain that you plugged into something beyond your wildest imaginings always result in a significant shift or transformation of some kind. It's as though you come into contact with a metaphorical third rail. A surge of energy flows through you, and you realize that the gods have touched you.

Think about it for a moment. Here you are contemplating a goal and considering just how you can achieve it. Or you know you must come up with a new approach since all previous efforts have fallen far short of success. Or like my brother, you simply feel compelled to take the road less travelled. Regardless of how you got to the moment when your *Passion* stirred and your *Imagination* lit up like a flare so you could see a future as if it were now, you are ready to act, to actually make the future become now.

What are the tools you'll need to achieve your *Vision*? Is your dream of an organization in which all people relate with respect? Then what will you do to begin that process? You might create a detailed strategy that includes a communication plan for getting others onboard. Regardless of the steps you take, standing still is not an option unless you are willing to settle for having had a hallucination.

Perhaps your vision is of a new product or service that your team could provide, or you're focusing on creating a piece of art, or music, or furniture. In this stage of *Creativity,* you begin by assembling the raw materials that you'll require. What tools, equipment, sponsors, allies, funding, and time will you need so you can form something that you saw in your mind's eye and that has never existed in space and time? And as I said previously, everything that you see and experience sprouted from someone's imagination and became real through a creative process. Now you are a creator.

Inventiveness is sometimes mundane and other times brilliant. Each time someone generates something that didn't exist before, they are drinking from the well of human possibility that has nourished us from the beginning of our individual and collective existence. Creation arises from many different types of impulses. Sometimes it comes from the beautiful and the good that we usually consider when we think of the outcomes of *Passion* and *Imagination.* It can also be objects, sounds, and experiences borne of need or to ease our pain or discomfort.

Consider, for example, the difference in aesthetics between a common stool and an Eames lounge chair. Both fulfill our human need to take some weight off our feet. One is more utilitarian, and the other is more like a piece of art. Regardless which one you prefer, both items materialized through the creative process.

You will inspire others once you develop the capacity to appreciate the intricacies of human resourcefulness and *Creativity* whether in a stool, a pencil, or a nail *as well as* more sublime creations like a Stradivarius, Handel's Messiah, a Chihuly glass sculpture, or a single malt scotch. Each of these items is a creation and has become remarkable because someone remained open to the impulses that aroused their heart and then followed through to become a creator.

Because of the consuming nature of many leadership roles in our organizations, many individuals give very little time and energy to making something new. Many seem to be content with having become a highly paid and titled technician. However, that career path is not likely to expand your *Capacity for Innovation* or cause someone else to be touched, moved, or inspired by your endeavors. As an Inside*OUT* leader, you will want to become aware, receptive, and fluent in the technique, art, and science of leading others. You must be curious about creating the processes and environment in which others flourish. Leaders create the culture of the organization. You're the one who is responsible for creating the places and systems that will support other's ability to create, or you may inadvertently stifle their potential contributions. And even though we're discussing your capacities and competencies, remember that all this isn't ultimately about you. It's about them, your team, your employees, and your followers. It's the engendering leader who inspires the possible in others so that they will say, "I can do that!"

None of my clients were in industries we typically associate with creativity, such as film, dance, or music. Instead, they represented finance, publishing, manufacturing, healthcare, and education. In our culture, we usually don't think of these industries as flowing with creative juices. We have a bias about where to find creativity that does not serve us. We limit our collective potential by seeing our society divided along the lines of the creators and the doers.

However, every industry and field of endeavor requires creative responses to challenges and possibilities. There are creative people in every role in every organization. As a leader, you are the vital link for making certain this energy is unleashed for the benefit of your own organizations and for our larger communities.

In fact, there now exist entire organizations that are made up of iconoclasts, individuals who see things *not for what one thinks they are, but for what they might be.* The need for more effective solutions in our society is so great that some individuals have linked arms by creating consulting groups to forge innovative solutions to existing needs. IDEO, a Palo Alto design firm with a global influence, is one such group. Tim Brown, CEO of IDEO, writes about their process.

> What we need are new choices—new products that balance the needs of individuals and of society as a whole; new ideas that tackle global challenges of health, poverty, and education; new strategies that result in differences that matter and a sense of purpose that engages everyone affected by them. It is hard to imagine a time when the challenges we faced so vastly exceeded the creative resources we have brought to bear on them.[15]

This organization is in the business of innovating, creating, and generating ideas that support their clients as well as the planet. Plus, they teach others how they do it too.

Once you have opened your heart and your eyes to your own *Creativity,* your next step, as a leader, is to infuse innovation throughout your organization. In this way, you expand what you alone have been capable of, and you become the inspirational force for possibility that will be picked up by others in the organization. This is how you launch your *Vitality.* You don't do this for yourself, because remember, its not about you.

Vitality

Vitality means that you are an essential and integral source of energy for your organization. As a vital leader, your emphasis is on bringing forth stuff and then sustaining what has been created. This stage in the *Capacity for Innovation* assures that both your ideas and those of others get support, nourishment, and promotion because you are staying in touch with your *Passion*, that stage of *Inspiration* that began as an inner fire. This sustaining quality guarantees that you remain a source for manifesting the possible. This life force gives breath to a fresh flow of possibilities, not just a singular occurrence. *Vitality* is what happens when you build a culture of innovation. It has a way of continually inspiring you and your team. It creates a kind of perpetual motion.

The animating principle of *Vitality* requires you to maintain an open heart and mind. This means not just being open to the exciting breakthrough moments but also open to the struggles that appear in your organization. Not all births are without labor. As you and those around you forge more creative ways of responding to business challenges and organizational possibilities, you will need to be open about your concerns and mostly about the feelings you are having about the process and outlook. This is not a time to paint rosy pictures or to try to inspire your team by telling them how they should act.

As you establish new ways of organizing yourselves, there will definitely be moments of doubt and worry. Not everyone will be on the same page. Some will cling to the familiar ways of operating. Those old ways feel safe because they are already known, and venturing forward without certainty is scary for most people. You might even be frightened yourself. That's okay; just admit it to your team and invite them to join you in facing the questions and uncertainties that are sure to show up. Remember, *Inspiration* begins with *Passion* so don't forget to let yours show.

I suppose every generation feels like their situation is uniquely challenging, but we're now in the midst of a tsunami. We're currently experiencing unprecedented complexity in our organizations due to an accelerating global spread of technology. And many of the challenges we're facing are exceptional in both scale and complexity. They require a kind of leading that is correspondingly unparalleled. We already know that the leader who continues to maintain structures and processes using existing techniques will be ineffective in these complicated situations.

Ron Heifetz, founding director of the Center for Public Leadership at the Harvard Kennedy School, describes *technical* leaders as those who are skilled at deploying proven solutions to typical problems using known strategies and responses. This describes good managers, and there will always be a need for this disciplined individual in organizations. Although, when you expand your leadership repertoire to deal with the never-before-seen challenges, *adaptive* leading will require you to admit that the challenge is multifaceted and unfamiliar beyond your dreams and your experience. Rather than exhibiting a deer-in-the-headlights reaction, you'll need to sincerely declare that you're committed to finding a way through the maze and that you're recruiting everyone in the organization to help in getting to the other side. As a leader who is taking the adaptive approach, you cannot rely on your expertise or on your authority. You will have to depend on your ability to inspire others to adapt and to join you in tackling the challenge at hand.

In order to grow in this stage of *Vitality*, you must remain agile in problem solving and exercise all of your *Imagination* and *Creativity* when addressing emerging challenges. Innovative solutions call for adaptation in your responses and for you to bring your people along to the frontier of possibility in your organization.

Here's how IDEO has adapted to provide innovative solutions. In order to solve complex problems and to find desirable solutions for their clients, their designers use a methodology they call "design thinking." Their in-house teams draw upon logic, imagination, intuition, and systemic reasoning when exploring possibilities for solutions they could propose as outcomes that benefit their customers. Then someone got another creative idea, they methodized their design thinking process so they could train individuals from other organizations, teaching others how to become innovators themselves, making the IDEO team unnecessary. Except that's not all. They also created an entire division of the company that is now IDEO U so anyone can learn from them through online courses.

The fact that IDEO not only employs design thinking in their practice but also packages it for others to use is exactly what I mean by *Vitality*. This innovative energy perpetuates and multiplies when an organization like IDEO spawns new centers of innovation within client organizations. It reminds me of the proverb, "Give a man a fish, and you feed him for a day. Teach a man to fish, and you feed him for a lifetime." As a leader with an expanding *Capacity for Innovation,* you'll be seeking ways to generate zones of creativity and innovation in your own organization and to do so in unheard of ways.

Assembling individuals from widely different disciplines to tackle a challenge is one of the most unusual and productive ways to ensure that you will sustain the notion of innovation. You can do this for personal issues, like a career move or the landscape design of your apartment terrace, or you can apply it to organizational challenges, like infusing the attitude of customer service throughout the organization or creating a more private experience for patients at your clinic. Bringing together a group of individuals from diverse disciplines will yield ideas that you could never have achieved on your own.

Tim Brown describes the benefit of getting input from a diverse design team. "A competent designer can always improve on last year's new widget, but an interdisciplinary team of skilled design thinkers is in a position to tackle more complex problems. From pediatric obesity to crime prevention to climate change, design thinking is now being applied to a range of challenges that bear little resemblance to the covetable objects that fill the pages of today's coffee-table publications."[16]

In order for you, as an Inside*OUT* leader, to sustain your *Capacity for Innovation* within yourself and within your organization, you will need to broaden your own perspective repeatedly. Back in the chapter on Identity, you discovered, and perhaps even named, several of your key parts, your subpersonalities. And throughout this book, you're discovering ways to expand other parts of yourself. Thus, you will be uniquely prepared for this stage in your development of *Inspiration*. You will find that the more you innovate the more diverse you will become. Your abilities, interests, knowledge, and resourcefulness will continue to expand, and you will become a fountain of *Vitality* for your team, your organization, and your community.

A focused way to think about this approach is to envision different personas. The good folks at IDEO have come up with what they refer to as *Ten Faces of Innovation*. They've identified these different types of contributors as key to actually implementing an idea. They're passionate about pairing ideas with action as seen by the names they give to each of the ten roles: Anthropologist, Experimenter, Cross-Pollinator, Hurdler, Collaborator, Director, Experience Architect, Set Designer, Caregiver, and Storyteller.[17]

Becoming this kind of multi-faceted leader illustrates the variety of perspectives needed when you truly undertake to innovate, not merely improve or fix. Regardless, if these different roles are embodied in just a few individuals or if you're fortunate enough to have each role assigned to a different person, what remains is the value of making your problem-solving team expansive enough to include each of these perspectives on innovation and their unique contribution.

As you ripen in your sensitivities to being inspired and to become inspiring, you'll experience a sort of steady flow of energy because you are vital, life giving, and life affirming. At times, the substance that makes up your imaginings, your *Vision* and your *Creativity,* will simply flow. It's as if you're showered with this energy, and all you need to do is to open your heart, eyes, and arms to receive the gifts. And yet other times the tap isn't delivering anything. You show up, you turn on the tap, you wait, and nothing flows. You're tempted to throw in the towel, except the stuff that inspires is not necessarily a continual flow. It is now that your commitment to being available is steady, to sit patiently by the source.

Back in 1878, in a letter to his benefactress, the composer Tchaikovsky wrote about his own experience of waiting for stimulation.

> Do not believe those who try to persuade you that composition is only a cold exercise of the intellect. The only music capable of moving and touching us is that which flows from the depths of a composer's soul when he is stirred by inspiration. There is no doubt that even the greatest musical geniuses have sometimes worked without inspiration. This guest does not always respond to the first invitation.
>
> We must always work, and a self-respecting artist must not fold his hands on the pretext that he is not in the mood. If we wait for the mood, without endeavoring to meet it halfway, we easily become indolent and apathetic. We must be patient, and believe that inspiration will come to those who can master their disinclination.
>
> A few days ago I told you I was working every day

without any real inspiration. Had I given way to my disinclination, undoubtedly I should have drifted into a long period of idleness. But my patience and faith did not fail me, and today I felt that inexplicable glow of inspiration of which I told you; thanks to which I know beforehand that whatever I write today will have power to make an impression, and to touch the hearts of those who hear it.[18]

Are you able to ready yourself with pen in hand, or with your brush already dipped in paint, or with the notion of a more robust and enlightened team and then simply wait for the muse to touch, move, and inspire you? Are you able to repeat this readiness numerous times until you are touched? Quite simply, are you able to muster the patience? And once you are touched, will you then supply yourself with energy so that, in turn, you become the inspiration for others to reach beyond their own limits?

Coda

Maria will probably never compose a symphonic work regardless of how long she awaits the muse to inspire her. Nevertheless, what she achieved was similar to a fine piece of music. Her team came together, and each member now works in concert with the other department heads instead of in their previous solo performances.

She responded to her memory of the passion generated by the work of her young friend in Central America, her muse. She remembered and reconnected with her own innovative textile artistry. She corrected her reflex to focus on "administrivia" and instead took the longer view of where she wanted her organization to be and how she wanted her team to work together. And she courageously put her new insights on the line with her Board of Directors. This resulted in their own spine-growing evolution, and they rallied around her vision for the enterprise. In fairness to the Board's own development, they also recognized their need to step up, and they reorganized with an entirely new executive committee taking the reins.

Over the following years, Maria led her organization into first-in-the-region advances in medical technology, in innovative payer plans that became the model that several states adopted in the ongoing efforts for universal healthcare, in increased profitability for stakeholders, and in huge gains in employee and patient satisfaction. She innovated on so many fronts yet what amazed me was her own transformation from a sternly driven executive to a strong, compassionate, and creative leader.

It has been nearly ten years since she first contacted me, and she is no longer the Executive Director for that multi-state healthcare organization. She took the exit package she was offered after a national conglomerate purchased her very attractive organization. She used that occasion to take a year off from professional work to await the muse and then accepted an invitation to become the chairperson of the Board of Directors of an international medical aid mission.

I bet the other Board members and the executives in her new organization have already come under her spell. That's the way it is when you're simply following your passion for your work and for the people you serve.

*Never mistake knowledge
for wisdom.
One helps you make
a living;
the other helps you
make a life.*

—Sandra Carey

6

INTELLIGENCE
Capacity for Perception

Damien

I received a phone call from Anne, the Director of Human Resources. I had worked with her on several other projects, and now she asked if I would consider coaching the Executive Director of Medical Affairs. Then she gave me the back-story.

She told me that Damien was quick, self-motivated, and self-reliant—traits that were necessary when the company was launched ten years earlier, and there were few formal processes, and everyone had a dotted line connection to everyone else.

Then a couple years later, the company fortified its financial future when federal regulators approved one of their innovative medical devices for release to the marketplace. This meant that the organization was in the process of quickly expanding, and its leadership personnel had to suddenly adjust their skills and habits in order to manage the increased numbers of staff.

Damien reported directly to the CEO in this small to medium sized company. He now had six direct reports and over twenty people in his group. Anne said that Damien was generally liked but that his early qualities were now causing some problems. She said that the CEO feared that Damien lacked the self-discipline or the ability to influence others in ways that could help the organization grow to its next level. And she added that the CEO had said that Damien would need to change or to move on since there were no upward or lateral moves available for him within the organization.

Anne told me how Damien would pop up anywhere, and at almost any meeting, even when he wasn't invited. He was like an irritating overseer, poking his nose into everyone else's business but seldom completing his own tasks. She said that ten years ago that was the way nearly everyone worked in what was then more like a boutique than a business.

I accepted the challenge. And before signing the contract, I requested a pre-coaching meeting with Damien. Both the client and I need to be confident that we can work together based on mutual regard, a level of comfort between the two of us, and suitability between the client's needs and my abilities.

I arranged to meet with Damien at a local coffee bar for a face-to-face meeting. I discovered that he was open, warm, and engaging. He conveyed most of the information that Anne had already given to me. He was sincere when he said that he wanted my help, and he didn't disappoint. After our first meeting, we both agreed to work together, and he went on to tackle his development with vigor and grace.

When I interviewed his peers and staff, I learned that they generally liked Damien but were especially irritated by the ways he deftly avoided accountability. Others said he argued for his points of view but didn't seem to care about theirs. He didn't always deliver on time yet would become impatient with others' delays. He tended to micro-manage and to insist on one right way. In fact, one of his peers even said that he was "narrow-minded." As it turned out, these observations were some of the same reasons for the CEO's ultimatum.

I kept hearing the phrase "narrow-minded" in my mind as we continued to work together. I really didn't get the idea that he was stubborn, as I would have expected, though there was something very gritty and down-to-earth about him. He was blunt and said it like he saw it: a quality that helped me know where he stood.

As we worked together, I just wasn't able to identify what was going on with him. Nothing seemed so egregious for which the CEO would want to dismiss him. And my interview with the CEO didn't give me any new substance, just more stories.

Then, during one of our meetings when we were looking into the feedback others gave about him and without any prompting, he took a dive into the deep end of the pool.

He said that as a young man he eventually accepted that he was intelligent, but growing up in very modest surroundings with parents who never attended high school and an older sibling who didn't complete high school, college had never been on his radar screen. He couldn't recall that the word "college" was ever spoken in his home. He said that if college had been mentioned it certainly wasn't held out as an option for him. It was simply mentioned as something other young people might do. The absence of his parents' interest in his higher education was no doubt driven in part by their own lack of formal education, in part from their humble economic and social status, and in part because Damien wasn't interested in college at that time.

He interrupted himself as he told me his story to say, "But to be fair, had I expressed any interest in college, I'm certain that my parents would've been delighted and done what they could to support my interests."

He added that his parents were curious people and that his dad had a small collection of books. His dad would frequently visit the local public library to read the latest news and science magazines. Damien remembered how much he enjoyed tagging along with his father on those visits where he absorbed those early impressions about the world and his dad's curiosity. He spoke respectfully as he reflected that his dad was clearly inquisitive and had educated himself through those frequent visits.

Then there was another experience that was to shadow him for many years. Near the end of his ninth grade, the principal and a counselor called him in to discuss his plans for the next year. Both of these thoughtful and genuinely caring administrators urged him to consider enrolling in the college prep curriculum for tenth grade even though he had previously been enrolled in a basic curriculum and his grades were just average—or below.

He was stunned. Perhaps they had the wrong guy. Then they pulled out *his* grade records. Oh, this'll be good, he thought. Let's see how they explain college prep to this marginally-making-it fifteen year old.

While there was little else he could recall about the meeting, he remembered that they said something about him not working up to his potential. The prospects of being with the popular and smart kids tickled his ego, and he stepped into what for him was to become the most challenging year of his young life.

Fast forward...he nearly failed the tenth grade and left humiliated and bitter. Then he spent his last two years of high school doing the absolute minimum required to gain a diploma. He made no effort toward his own fulfillment, and he expressed no respect or appreciation for the outstanding school and his excellent teachers. He now felt ashamed that he had wasted such a wonderful resource.

Okay, his was a sad and interesting story, but what was going on? Why did he tell me all this especially when we're trying to work together to help him grow into, and keep, his job? Damien was one of those people who just didn't seem to fit the systems, and it took him many years to discover his own path to higher education. He completed his undergraduate degree when he was twenty-seven years old and already a father of two small children. After several different career attempts and two more decades of birthdays, he had finally acquired his PhD.

He told me that throughout his university education he had to seek out the classes and learning methods that worked for him. He just needed to learn how to use his mind in a manner and setting unique to his intellectual wiring. Using traditional ways like reading a textbook, researching more documents to gather info, and writing papers just didn't work for him. And he had to always deal with his shame over his failures in high school and his inferiority towards schoolwork.

Eventually, he discovered that it was easier for him to take in information through dialogue rather than through reading. He found that he was much more suited to peer discussions, watching videos, and learning from a favored professor who seemed to understand him perfectly. When a professor presented a new principle or concept, Damien would grasp it more quickly if he could see the principle at work in another discipline. He discovered that he processed information best when he could use parallel learning or a multidisciplinary approach to problem solving.

"Ah-ha." There it was. This was why he was so open in telling me about himself. He needed to talk. And it was through talking that he did his best thinking. Our sessions went from one to two-hour meetings. He found it really difficult to do much self-study outside of our sessions. He clearly worked best when we were in conversation. I began to see him as a dialogical learner.

It was especially exciting for me to work with Damien because as a coach I needed to constantly reconfigure my input or resources so he could grasp and retain the material. For me he quickly became much more multi-dimensional and interesting. And I never again heard the phrase "narrow-minded" from his colleagues. In fact, I noticed how frequently he spoke using analogies or metaphors to explain something.

When we would discuss a method or a skill, he learned quickly. He loved to wrestle with ideas and suggestions. And it was in moments like these that I could imagine his work colleagues rolling their eyes and thinking that here was that stubborn Damien again. Yet I never found him stubborn. I found him compassionate because he was adamant that information be presented in many different ways so that more people could understand it. He had become an advocate for his and for other's intellectual diversity.

Sometimes, he would stand up and walk around when he was talking: it was as if he needed to move his body for his mind to work. And on occasion, I would squint my eyes and imagine that I was watching a dancer work out his choreography. It was beautiful to observe. Here was someone who was cognitively very intelligent, but he was not versatile in using the many other ways of perceiving his world.

In fact, part way through the coaching contract, I did something that I had never done before with a coaching client. Damien was not able to grasp some of the nuances of the skills and the leadership processes that we discussed. Consequently, I proposed to him that we find a way for me to provide some just-in-time coaching during actual team meetings.

He scheduled an informal meeting with his entire staff so he could tell them what we had in mind. He spoke directly and confidently to his team. He started by describing what he was learning about how he processed information and why he wanted to use some of their actual working meetings as a place for him to get real-time coaching from me. We all agreed that this would certainly be a novel approach. The team was on-board and so we embarked on the experiment.

The meetings began to look and sound more like a group of highly motivated university students with their benevolent professor than an actual workplace meeting. Damien quickly blossomed in this new format, and it wasn't long before I no longer participated and he continued to sponsor work conversations throughout his department whether he facilitated them or not.

He told me later that the team was actually working together now by using this open and conversation-based project lab approach in most of its work.

He was a rapid learner, and I was eager to work with him to help him discover additional ways to take in information and to practice how he could, in turn, vary the ways he would deliver on his leadership tasks.

Intelligence: Capacity for Perception

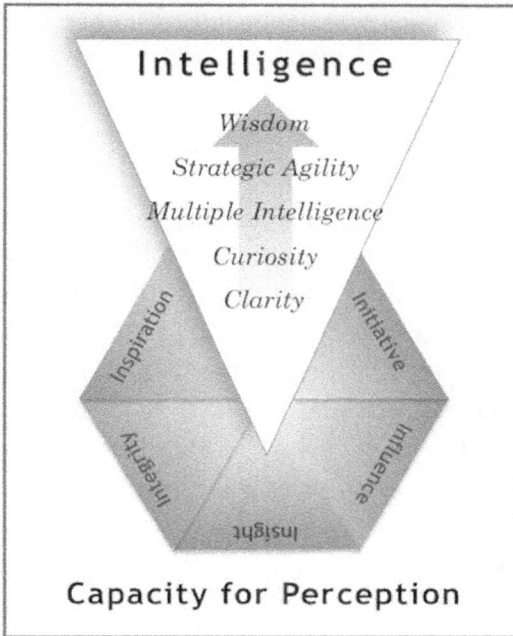

Intelligence is the capacity for using all of your perceptive abilities. Though this capacity requires sophisticated mental functioning, it also arouses and employs all the other perceptive channels available for becoming fully human.

Developing this capacity will probably take more time and patience than others. Yet the effort you invest here will result in significant collateral benefit among all your other leadership capacities. Remember, "a rising tide lifts all boats."

The themes of intellect and education are completely interwoven in our Western society, and I'm conscious of how they played out in my life. Some of Damien's story could have been my own. That is why I'm fascinated by how people learn and how each of us must become aware of how we take in information, how we process it, and how we apply what we know.

Sir Ken Robinson, an engaging, witty, scholarly professor, and occasional TED speaker says this.

We need to radically rethink our view of intelligence. We know three things about intelligence. One, it's diverse. We think about the world in all the ways that we experience it. We think visually, we think in sound, we think kinesthetically. We think in abstract terms, we think in movement.

Secondly, intelligence is dynamic. If you look at the interactions in the human brain, intelligence is wonderfully interactive. The brain isn't divided into compartments. In fact, creativity—which I define as the process of having original ideas that have value—more often than not, comes about through the interaction of different disciplinary ways of seeing things.

And the third thing about intelligence is, it's distinct. I believe our only hope for the future is to adopt a new conception of human ecology, one in which we start to reconstitute our conception of the richness of human capacity.[1]

Ah, there's that notion of *capacity* again. So let's dig deeper to explore how you can develop this container for knowing rather than the specifics of its content, especially considering how this relates to leadership.

Expansion is a subtext throughout this entire book, so it's appropriate to launch this part of the material with the same concept.

Neuroplasticity is the way the brain expands its capability. Plasticity is most often referred to when a person suffers a loss of function in an area of the brain. This loss may result from injury, stroke, or disease. In some circumstances, this marvelous organ adjusts to this loss by delegating some of its functions to areas that were not damaged.

Elizabeth Landau, contributor for CNN in an article about U.S. Congresswoman, Gabrielle Giffords, who was critically injured in an assassination attempt in 2011, writes, "We know now that it is possible to form new brain cells called neurons even in adulthood. By doing rehab to relearn basic tasks, a patient with traumatic brain injury may be able to form new brain connections that allow him or her to move and talk again. How well the patient recovers depends on the severity of the damage, but substantial progress can be made in some cases."[2]

Except, the rest of us don't need to wait until we would undergo a brain injury in order to experience plasticity. There is an increasing body of research and clinical practice that points to actions humans can take to expand their brain functions using mental exercises, as well as physical exercise, to promote the development of new neurons.

Practicing a physical skill *in your mind*, such as a golf swing or a formal presentation, can produce the same changes in the brain's systems as you would see if you had actually performed the physical activity. Many athletes and musicians use imagination and visualization techniques to prepare for their peak performances.

Recently, while watching the World Alpine Skiing Championships, I saw a downhill skier waiting at the top of the mountain before her run. She was standing with her arms slightly outstretched in front of her just like when she skis. Her eyes were closed, and her head bobbed slightly from side to side. I was most impressed by the almost imperceptible movements in her body as she skied down the hill in her mind, preparing for the experience of actually skiing the slope. I wonder what changes you might experience if you employed active imagination and visualization in preparation for your leadership interactions?

Chade-Meng Tan is a leader who imagined something unique. He was one of Google's earliest engineers (employee #107), and more recently, served on Google's Talent Team. He brought his personal practice of mindfulness to the organization. In his book, *Search Inside Yourself*, he describes how, with the aid of a small team, he formed an entire group at Google to answer the question, "What if contemplative practices can be made beneficial both to people's careers and to business bottom lines?"[3] He designed a course for Google's most talented individuals. His intention was to transform how people worked and how the organization prospered.

Back in the early 1990s, when I first began to explore how to bring the notions of reflection and mindfulness into the business environment, I faced the challenge of terminology—especially how to refer to something that carried what some may have heard as spiritual overtones into the existing business culture. Corporate language was all about effectiveness, profitability, transactions, and market-share. At the time, I wasn't savvy enough to find a way to translate what I was imagining into my daily work. Yet after a day of work and over dinner with my colleagues, we would talk openly about deeply meaningful experiences, feelings, and perspectives. Then the next morning, back inside the client's environment, we closeted what was most dear to us, and we interacted once again with our clients and spoke of communication skills required for managerial effectiveness. We simply didn't yet have the language to go any deeper within the corporate environment.

On a few occasions, I had the privilege of conducting workshops in religious or educational organizations, and I realized how much freer I was to use language that bridged the organizational and the contemplative worlds. Then, as I expanded my own capacities, I became more resourceful with unpacking language that described the complexities of the human heart and mind. Back in the corporate settings, I began to experiment with using vernacular that spanned the culture of business and the recent discoveries about the human mind and spirit.

As the 1990s rolled on, more writers travelled across that language bridge resulting in a much more open and integrative approach to human development in many organizations. By the early 2000's, bookstores and poster art in corporate offices reflected the widespread endorsement of the mystical with the organizational. And then came TED Talks and podcasts. This social evolution has benefitted both individuals and organizations. As I see it, there are many benefits from practicing mindfulness exercises; such as focus, the ability to concentrate and not allow minor distractions to divert your attention; choice, the mental space to select your actions rather than automatically reacting—hugely important in interpersonal interactions; and resilience, the ability to bounce back from unexpected, real, or perceived life and work events.

The value of mindfulness is no longer simply anecdotal. Harvard-affiliated researchers in the *Mindfulness-Based Stress Reduction Program* have concluded, "It is fascinating to see the brain's plasticity and that, by practicing meditation, we can play an active role in changing the brain and can increase our well-being and quality of life."[4]

By analyzing MRIs (magnetic resonance images), the researchers have "found increase gray-matter density in the hippocampus, known to be important for learning and memory, and in structures associated with self-awareness, compassion, and introspection."[5] And these benefits occurred from simply meditating an average of 27 minutes a day for eight weeks.

There is now a wealth of studies and scholarly examples that support the benefits of mindfulness. And this emerging knowledge is being included in many human resource and organizational development programs. However, some leaders are not yet prepared to take their mind to the gym for a thoughtful workout.

As a leader, your daily life is full of events that challenge you, including when some employees seem to be playing for the other team. There's the staff person who is not prepared for the client meeting, an email announcing a lost bid or a need to cut staff, a supplier's change of specs or delivery date, the discovery of questionable activities by people inside the organization, marketing attacks from competitors, or even a call from your child's school requesting your response to yet one more wrinkle in an otherwise lovely day.

If this describes you, you may be prone to react to stressful circumstances in ways that could negatively threaten both the goals leading to the bottom line as well as the relationships that you need in order to maintain a profitable outcome. Damien wasn't especially stressed out by turmoil like this. He simply did his best to figure it all out on his own. But it was the way he went about it that stressed everyone around him. Over the time I've known Damien, he has gone from being someone who was first described as narrow-minded to being a leader who was well on his way to becoming broad-minded. In this chapter, we'll explore more about how leaders can expand their *Capacity for Perception* by consciously utilizing their many kinds of *Intelligence*. In this way, a leader can experience and exhibit full-mindedness as a way to navigate the oft times bumpy organizational terrain.

The five stages in developing your *Capacity for Perception* begin with the internal experiences of *Clarity* and *Curiosity*. Then we'll delve into the world of *Multiple-Intelligence* before we discuss *Strategic Agility* and sum up this chapter by exploring *Wisdom*.

Clarity

Intelligence requires a keen mental focus that results in inner lucidity. This experience of being clear of mental murkiness is more than the profound absence of confusion. It is characterized by the ability to notice a single idea or item amidst a sea of other possibilities that are also clamoring for your attention.

Clarity is similar to the function of the deck prism I talked about in chapter 1. It allows for available light to be gathered and then directed into unlit areas. Your aptitude with clarity will permit you to sort through the murky data that often comes in your direction from competing and disparate sources within and outside your organization.

Have you ever wondered how a maestro can sort out the sound of an oboe while the rest of the orchestra is playing a passage as well? Or how a President or a prime minister can simultaneously deal with the huge number of important and urgent issues while seeming to single-mindedly attend to one key concern? Or what mental muscle must an Executive Director access to direct her staff to the fourth quarter action plan instead of succumbing to the constant and interrupting calls from an anxious Board member?

Daniel Goleman, journalist and author of *Emotional Intelligence*, writes, "A primary task of leadership is to direct attention. To do so, leaders must learn to focus their own attention. When we speak about being focused, we commonly mean thinking about one thing while filtering out distractions."[6]

And that one thing you must focus on could be something entirely about you, or something about others, or even something that encompasses the wider world. Just because you direct attention to one thing does not imply it is small or simple.

Identifying and maintaining focus, or *Clarity*, certainly employs one's *Will*. And in the next chapter on *Initiative* you'll examine the role that volition plays in a leader's capacities. For now though, let's dig a bit deeper into the experience of *Clarity* so your intentions have something to grab on to while at the same time you're expanding your overall capacity for leading.

The efforts you make to increase your *Clarity* will be most effective when you nourish your body. *Clarity* occurs when you are well rested. Getting plenty of sleep is apparently quite under-valued by most organizations. With smartphone connectivity, global engagements demanding attention at times other than nine-to-five in your own time zone, unreasonable expectations and quotas that multiply like bunnies, and a twenty-first century culture in America that considers availability 24/7 the norm, it's no wonder that so many people get burned up and burned out.

Very few employers in the U.S. will encourage you to unplug—to take time out for just you. Fewer will actively monitor the demands on personal time and health of their high-grade employees. It's up to you to set limits, to be clear with others about your personal boundaries.

You may be like many of my clients who describe their list of priorities like this: their job receives their primary attention, their spouse might come in second, or perhaps their children are second and then their spouse gets bumped to a lower tier of importance. Then, if there is time, civic engagement and volunteer work might appear on their calendar or on their wish list. And as if this isn't tragic enough, what is missing from this equation is the care and nourishment of themselves. Sleep, food, and regular exercise are important for physical fitness but even more necessary for mental fitness—which just happens to be the engine for most of a leader's actual work.

You probably will not need marathon-running stamina in order to perform your duties, but you certainly need a clear mind. In order to get your followers to enthusiastically engage in an endeavor, you must first develop and possess a deeply held inner focus. Out-of-shape leaders do not merit the followership of others. Others will not respect the directions of those who do not take their own counsel—who don't take care of themselves inside and out.

Clarity, or focus, is a state of mind. It's great when it can be experienced in the absence of distraction, but your *Clarity* is more likely to be needed *in spite of* distraction. When you can sit in the eye of the storm with others' fears and demands swirling around you and maintain clear sight, hearing, and a sense of yourself, as well as others and the larger world in which you are held, then you have realized the ultimate benefit of *Clarity*.

Clarity is not so much the absence of distortion, but rather it is your mind's ability to establish a direct line of sight that pierces through the fog. One of the ways to expand this capacity is to shift from reflexively reacting to the clamoring calls around you by simply noticing what is going on and quieting your impulse to act. Once you're still, you'll then arrive at the place where you can begin to open your mind just a bit to the unrelenting itch of inquisitiveness.

Curiosity

Inside*OUT* leaders must learn how to use their curiosity rather than to be at the mercy of its unpredictable whims. Psychologist Robert Rosen, in his work *Grounded: How Leaders Stay Rooted in an Uncertain World,* writes, "The main ingredient of intellectual health is what we call deep curiosity. Humans are curious by nature but it's the 'deep' part that marks effective leadership. This kind of curiosity is intentional, and it hones in on the knowns and unknowns as part of an ongoing personal education, one that a leader pursues rigorously and regularly. Deep curiosity fundamentally shapes our answers to the 'Who are you?' question."[7] And you can use this fundamental tool for discovering who others are as well.

Curiosity means loosening your attachment to one right way, your way. Children are full of curiosity because they have not yet attached themselves to opinions. As a curious leader, you'll need to engage with others and with what's possible for them by exploring what's beyond their recognized comfort zones. You'll observe not just how others act, but more importantly, you'll explore why they feel and think the way they do—what it is that's driving their behavior.

You'll become more intelligent as you increase your field of awareness. And you'll get smarter by constantly pushing into the unknown and then seeking ways to engage and learn from your encounters, instead of settling for a narrow set of answers. *Curiosity* is the tool for preventing an overly rigid and righteous perspective.

I recall dining with several coworkers and guests at the home of the founder of the company where I once worked. This executive seemed genuinely interested in other people. After everyone around the table was served, he would toss a question into the conversation, something like, "What are you most looking forward to next month?" Invariably, there would be the predictable clever remark from one or two guests before someone else would offer a more deeply held expectation. All the gems of our previously hidden thoughts went unnoticed prior to the host's curious question. Then the collective dinner party dropped an octave to a more resonant tone—a sound much closer to everyone's heart. By asking a simple question, the entire evening's discussion turned toward more meaningful topics.

Asking curious questions means you don't already know the answers. And it's also not using a question to make a statement. Somehow, for many of us, we learned to express our opinion by asking questions that have obvious answers. Perhaps it was your mother and father who, when you first came home from school and dropped your books on the floor, asked, "Is that where your backpack belongs?"

Your parents already knew where your school bag was to be placed. They asked because they wanted at least two things: your backpack put away and you developing a habit for order and responsibility. Little did they realize that a different habit was being taught—asking *non*-curious questions.

Perhaps you, or your manager, have also asked questions like these:

"Why did you do that?"

"What were you thinking?"

"Didn't you think that I would need to know?"

"When was I supposed to find out?"

We reflexively ask questions like these instead of simply stating that we're surprised or shocked by the other person's actions. Meanwhile, we genuinely might not know the answers to these questions, but the interrogation is intended to express our feelings of anger, surprise, fear, etc., and perhaps to trip up the poor person on the other end. These sorts of questions deplete trust and rarely increase our knowledge.

One of the reasons why so many leaders are the last to discover crucial information, that would have helped them to make earlier and wiser decisions, is because many leaders live in a bubble of power that others find intimidating and that potentially causes employees to delay and withhold bad news. Leaders who are genuinely curious are more likely to receive critical information that's delivered voluntarily, even if the information incriminates the messenger.

A gulf can occur between you and your followers if you're micro managing, or if you're perceived as bullying by shaming or attacking, or even if you're remaining distant in order to avoid the first two. Regardless of your tactics, the result is your creation of an organization with sheep-like followers where knowledge and innovation are closely guarded commodities and not likely to be shared. Organizations like these are certainly not known for their breakthrough products, processes, or beloved leaders.

Nonetheless, you can expose your inquisitiveness to your team by being genuinely curious and seeking out what others already know while letting them be the problem-solvers. By putting your ego aside—the ego that wants to be seen as all-knowing—and by opening the floor to those who probably know better than you, you earn respect by giving respect.

In fact, if you ever received feedback that you appear to others to have all the answers and could benefit from greater humility, start asking questions—questions to which you personally don't have a clue as to the answer. Voluntarily put yourself in the place of a learner. Or you might also try to practice humility by exploring a dormant interest like photography or learning to play an instrument—anything that places you at the beginning of knowledge, in a place of "not knowing." *Curiosity* is one of the best mental tools for expanding your *Intelligence.*

What parts of you get stretched when you become curious and seek out the unknown?

Multiple Intelligences

Leading, as well as living, by deliberately exercising all parts of your intellectual capacity become training for developing your intellect. But many of us who grew up in the twentieth century were only aware of one way to get smarter—we were to study and apply ourselves to our schoolwork. And the measure of our success was one type of assessment administered several times during our education. The test results assigned a score that indicated only one measure of intelligence from low to high. Most of us probably scored in the broad average (normal IQ) range.

You might have had an experience similar to Damien's. Did you ever get the impression that you might be among the high average, or even gifted, population? Or did you ever fail to perform up to your own or someone else's standards for intelligence? Then just perhaps your "failure" was less about your intellectual performance and more about the understanding and practice of what constituted intelligence and how it was measured back then.

For many years, there has been a standard intelligence test for children and a different one for adults. These tests have been adjusted and normed periodically so the results reflect the continued advancement of individuals in a changing society. And to be fair, these tests have done a pretty good job of providing guidance for school and job placement.

Then in the late 1970s and early 80s, researchers, educators, and others began to stretch the boundaries of how we define intelligence. One person, Howard Gardner, brought a keen insight and much needed structure to help identify the multiple ways that individuals process information and make sense of their environment.

First of all, Gardner believed that for intelligence testing to be valid individuals had to *demonstrate* their intelligence and not just *talk* about it—as in responding to questions on a test form. Sitting down with a #2 pencil and selecting possible answers on a piece of paper or answering an interviewer's prompts about geographical directions isn't the same as actually using a map and compass to find your way through a maze.

Gardner's major contribution to the field of intelligence was to originally identify eight specific areas of intelligence that he believed encompass the human experience. Here is how he described each of them.

- *Linguistic:* An ability to analyze information and create products involving oral and written language such as speeches, books, and memos.
- *Logical-mathematical:* An ability to develop equations and proofs, make calculations, and solve abstract problems.
- *Spatial:* An ability to recognize and manipulate large-scale and fine-grained spatial images.
- *Musical:* An ability to produce, remember, and make meaning of different patterns of sound.

- *Bodily-kinesthetic:* An ability to use one's own body to create products or solve problems.
- *Naturalistic:* An ability to identify and distinguish among different types of plants, animals, and weather formations that are found in the natural world.
- *Intrapersonal:* An ability to recognize and understand his or her own moods, desires, motivations, and intentions.
- *Interpersonal:* An ability to recognize and understand other people's moods, desires, motivations, and intentions.[8]

Gardner's work will certainly prompt you and any other conscientious leader to consider and investigate the areas of intellect that you've been ignoring. Unfortunately, many aspiring leaders remain stuck by being smart in only one way, the way education and/or their supervisors have taught them. Though a twentieth century understanding of intelligence is necessary, it's not sufficient for leading in the twenty-first century. Analog leading will not survive in the complex digital environment of global and cross-cultural dynamics.

Today, you must employ all of your ways of knowing so that you can truly lead instead of merely perform. I urge you to challenge yourself by exploring your less familiar intelligences. This will require humility and vulnerability—traits also essential for twenty-first century leadership.

Most executives I've worked with appear to operate by primarily using only two types of intelligence: linguistic and logical-mathematical. And some leaders, those who utilize higher forms of social capital, seem to be in touch with their interpersonal intellect as well. The challenge for you is to explore and exercise the entire scope of possible intelligences. To do so would require you to dedicate yourself to a sort of mental cross training—in the same way that varied physical exercise develops strength, endurance, and agility.

On a personal note, ever since I became aware of this field of *Multiple Intelligences*, I have challenged myself to stretch into some of my own less-developed ways of perceiving. Though I can carry a tune reasonably well, at least when I sing Happy Birthday or other well-known songs, I bought a ukulele and spent many hours practicing, extending my understanding of notes, keys, and chords. I was not interested in becoming another Steve Martin, who took up the ukulele later in life, but I wanted to exercise an intellectual muscle that I wasn't using.

Neither my musical intellect, nor my kinesthetic intellect, which served me well in many athletic activities, could come to my rescue in dance. I always shrugged this off to the fact that I felt like I was dragging generations of pious Mennonite ancestors with me onto the dance floor. Okay, that's just an excuse since there is probably little correlation between my cultural background and my inability to dance.

Nevertheless, I stretched my willingness, and I explored dance. In fact, my wife and I included a brief waltz as part of our marriage ceremony because dance was so important to her. And more recently, my wife and I participated in a square dance club for several years. After hundreds of do-si-dos and allemande left patterns, I felt increasingly comfortable as my body moved to the rhythm of the music and the caller's guidance, and I became pretty good at it. And I bet you already figured out that I was relying on my logical and spatial intellect to master square dance patterns, instead of using a natural kinesthetic or musical intelligence.

I know of people who close themselves in a room, turn up the music, and let the rhythm and vibration move through them, letting their body move however it wishes. This can take you out of your mind as you experience the music and your body functioning as one. If you want to really stretch your kinesthetic intellect (along with lots of other parts of your psyche and body), consider an Argentine Tango dance marathon where two people who have never met before, and who will go their own way after 3-4 minutes of dance, step onto the floor and give themselves over to the music. The dancers look as if they've rehearsed for years though there is no previously planned pattern to their actions, just a willingness to become one element composed of their two beings and the music.

Since you're probably already fluent in linguistic and logical intelligences, you may be less inclined to explore the others, for example, naturalistic and musical intelligences. Having solid abilities in numerous intelligences is important for leading. Why, you ask? It's because you'll be developing a certain strength, endurance, and mental agility that will increase your concentration, endurance, and flexibility. In addition, you will be able to connect more effectively with followers who embody intelligences that are different from yours.

Since leading is primarily a social endeavor, you must expand your ways of perceiving by becoming most fluent in *intra*personal and *inter*personal intelligences.

These two ways of knowing are now widely known as "emotional intelligence," or shortened to EI or EQ. These particular intelligences have probably received the most attention of all the others due to the scholarly and articulate work of Daniel Goleman. He chose the phrase *Emotional Intelligence*, and by 1995, he used it as the title of his first book on the topic.

In his book, he describes the emotional competence framework as having two components, *personal competence*—how we manage ourselves using self-awareness, self-regulation, and motivation; and *social competence*—how we handle relationships, exercise empathy, and engage social skills to encourage desirable responses from others.[9] These relational intelligences, which show up in all human interactions, carry significant importance for you since leading is a type of tacit social agreement between you and your followers.

In his later book, *Primal Leadership,* Goleman went on to explore the connections between leadership and emotional intelligence. He describes the effects of emotions at work, both those that are expressed and used as well as those that are trapped and contained.

For too long the shop floor, corner office, and the boardroom have been places that were supposed to be emotionally sterile. We all narrowly assumed that there were only a very few feelings, like ambition and commitment, that were permitted in the workplace, and we didn't refer to them as "emotions."

I contend that the notion of an emotionally sterile workplace never existed because feelings and emotions are always present in human beings. But in this supposedly emotionally sterile environment, some workers experienced intimidation, disgust, and outrage. Leaders apparently felt they were only permitted to express certain feelings: those that perpetuated the environment of command and control. Oh no, we weren't emotional, were we?

Workplaces, not only people, also display an emotional mood. I recall my first meeting with a new client, Tom, at his office. I had done executive coaching in this company at several other locations both in America and Europe, but this one felt very different and odd. People were not walking around from office to office or chatting in the break room. Nor did the few I happened to encounter in the corridors or elevator even look at me. They shuffled among the cubicles with their heads down to avoid even the possibility of eye contact. There was a kind of quiet so profound that for a moment I wondered if it were a weekend morning. As a careful observer, I logged all this sensory data into my memory. This kind of data can become crucial in understanding a client's context during a coaching or consulting engagement.

One of my coaching client's major challenges was his advancement to the next step in his career. Though he certainly did himself no favors with his overly cautious style and awkwardly timed laughter, I discovered that his supervisor, the department head, was a bully (his description, not mine). I interviewed several of my client's peers to get their feedback about Tom's strengths and challenges. I also interviewed "the bully."

Well, no wonder there was silence and no one made eye contact. This department head embodied all the clichés of a tyrant. She spoke evenly and in a low voice, and her words were amputated before the last sounds left her lips. It was a very effective way to make me feel like I wasn't listening carefully enough, like I had a hearing or an attention problem. Her pattern of speech had the desired effect of causing me to lean in, to hang on her every word, in order to make sense of what she was saying.

When she wasn't busy looking elsewhere, she leaned back in her leather chair and glared at me across her half-lowered glasses. She didn't seem bored as much as irritated that I was occupying her time about something as trivial as the development of one of her senior executives. No wonder he had sought an outside coach; his boss was certainly not capable of showing her humanity. She expressed no interest in Tom's career.

Many studies—neurological, psychological, and sociological—have shown the impact that leaders have on people around them. My client was simply another exhibit A. This department head had so shaped the culture of her area that not only were her team members working under very stressful conditions, but the environment—sound, lighting, cubical arrangements, and even the aroma—had a stunning effect on me as a first time visitor. Can you imagine what it would be like to exchange forty to fifty hours of your life each week for the emotional pollution that a boss like this generates?

I'm sure you've had similar experiences in the workplace, places where others clouded the environment with their own toxicity. Were they places where moods were negative, where coworkers' health suffered, and the business became drudgery? Or perhaps you've had experiences where moods were high, communication was open, and people openly helped each other to achieve the goals of the team. You probably can recall how you felt working in those environments, how productive you were in favorable surroundings versus noxious ones. For that reason, as you lead, remember that your followers are counting on you to also set the emotional climate of the workplace and to create an open and trusting atmosphere for your team. Working in an organization is a communal endeavor with human beings who have feelings and who sometimes show those feelings in your work place. Are you attending to the climate of your team's surroundings?

This exploration of *Multiple Intelligence* would not be complete without one additional angle—the influence of values and ethics. Many are referring to this domain as "spiritual intelligence," or SQ. For the purpose of this discussion, let's define spiritual intelligence as an organizing and integrating function that connects and magnifies each of our other ways of knowing. That sounds almost like a maestro.

Gardner pointed out that it's necessary to *demonstrate* intelligence and not just to be able *talk* about it. This is also true about spiritual intelligence. The test of being spiritually smart is how we act. Followers care much more about how their leaders act than about what they say or even what they believe. What happens when your actions don't match your words? Quite simply, people believe what you do regardless what you say.

One very practical approach for developing and expanding your spiritual intelligence is the work of Cindy Wigglesworth. As a former Exxon executive and now consultant and coach, she has identified twenty-one measurable skills of spiritual intelligence. She defines spiritual intelligence as "the ability to behave with wisdom and compassion, while maintaining inner and outer peace, regardless of the situation."[10]

Additionally, Wigglesworth and her colleagues have developed a statistically valid assessment tool to identify and measure spiritual intelligence. I've used the assessment to identify my specific skill levels and what steps I could further develop in order to expand my capabilities in SQ.

What happens after you develop your *Multiple Intelligence*, your many ways of knowing? Well, there's even more for you to discover and to employ. You're not merely an organism led by your intellect. You can experience even more complex ways of perceiving through your capacity for knowing.

Strategic Agility

Strategic Agility means that you can employ your multiple ways of perceiving as well as transform them into new knowledge and new value. You do this by creating, defining, and fluidly moving among possible future conditions. This capability is more than skillful planning. It means you're able to re-invent yourself, to reinvent your business, and thus to create tomorrow's endeavors. And you can even do this repeatedly.

This leadership ability is not only an adaptive response to changing circumstances, but it is also the ability to create and contribute to what is possible for an envisioned future with strategic action right from the start.

As you develop your various intellects, you will experience the benefits from your mental cross training. For example, you will begin to notice how you can perceive interrelationships among different aspects of a problem. The more experience you have in different disciplines, or in different industries, or even in different parts of the same organization, the more you will begin to have a broader understanding of the complex systems involved, and you can see new patterns. You might even find yourself borrowing from an observation you made in one discipline and applying it to another. At the same time, you'll become more fluent in the world's complex systems, and you'll gain greater understanding of how it works.

This *Strategic Agility* is a product of having developed a kind of cognitive interplay. You'll tend to internalize multiple fields of information and have a greater ability to observe and understand the connectivity among phenomena. It's the capability to see relationships among disparate fields of knowledge which greatly increases the odds of coming up with novel and valuable solutions.

One example of how this agility occurs is seen in the applications of nature to architecture and design. As Janinie Benyus of the Biomimicry Institute says, "Biomimicry is an approach to innovation that seeks sustainable solutions to human challenges by emulating nature's time-tested patterns and strategies. The core idea is that nature has already solved many of the problems we're grappling with. Animals, plants, and microbes are the consummate engineers. After billions of years of research and development, failures are fossils, and what surrounds us is the secret to survival."[11]

Among my clients, I noticed a recurring theme. Those emerging leaders who stepped out of their comfort zone of familiar professional know-how and took on a new assignment requiring a steep learning curve were the ones who advanced into senior leadership roles much more quickly than those who took a linear—safer and slower—path to advancement. And those who took on the responsibilities of a foreign assignment where both language and culture were added to the learning curve advanced even faster.

We can again learn from the metaphor of the orchestra that we explored back in chapter 2. In his book, *A Whole New Mind,* Daniel Pink describes it this way.

In any symphony, the composer and the conductor have a variety of responsibilities. They must make sure that the brass horns work in sync with the woodwinds, that the percussion instruments don't drown out the violas. But perfecting those relationships—important though is—is not the ultimate goal of their efforts. What conductors and composers desire—what separates the long remembered from a quickly forgotten—is the ability to marshal these relationships into a whole whose magnificence exceeds the sum of its parts...I prefer to think of it simply as seeing the big picture.[12]

So maestro, how are you doing with guiding your inner orchestra? Have you mastered the role of conductor or are you simply occupying the position? Can you hear both the nuances of the oboe as well as the grandeur of the orchestra? And do you have a clear sense of where your masterpiece is headed so that you can strategically conduct your own self to reach your envisioned finale?

But, you say, not so hasty. Isn't there more? Yes, there is one more treasure map I want to relate to you. Let me set the context. In my work, I've traveled throughout the United States, and in Latin America and Europe, and I feel privileged to have worked with many different companies, industries, and people. When I was on an assignment overseas and my workday was finished, I frequently sat down to eat and drink with my host clients as if we had been friends for a long time. One of the most rewarding aspects of these moments was when I would discover how similar we were as humans. We had similar concerns for our partners, our children, our countries, and our planet, plus I discovered that we often shared very similar values.

In these warm and friendly settings, I was often asked for my opinion about the news du jour as CNN or BBC was lighting up the world. My hosts were especially eager to talk about whichever U.S. President was currently occupying the

White House. Without fail, I would hear individuals describe a viewpoint about the U.S. that was unavailable to my ears when I was stateside. Their views were always refreshing because, although I might not share them, I was seeing how they might come to their conclusions from their vantage point. They were aware of the global influence of the U.S. in a way that Americans, for the most part, are unaware.

It wasn't until I shared a drink with individuals at a table spread with unfamiliar flavors and sights that I experienced our shared humanity. As the world gets smaller from a connectivity standpoint, we must engage from our best, our mutual *Strategic Agility*. We owe it not only to our careers and companies but also to all children around the planet who must take up the baton of leadership in the future.

Our world has always been overflowing with the different habits, beliefs, and cultural differences. And with the melting of glaciers also comes the need to dissolve our assumptions and biases. Many forms of technology—that we humans have created—are quickly propelling us all into a future for which we have little time to prepare.

Our many differences stand in stark contrast while at the same time our shared humanity appears on our doorsteps. And so, we are all presented with choices for how to relate more intelligently today so as to ensure more safe and sane tomorrows. You will need to employ your *Strategic Agility* if you are to successfully navigate the connections and the complexities of our shared global marketplace.

To equip us to deal with these new situations, Howard Gardner, in his book, *Five Minds for the Future,* has expanded his concept of *Multiple Intelligences.* He encourages us to look into the future with a compelling case for intelligences that we yet need to develop. He wrote.

In the interconnected world in which the vast majority of human beings now live, it is not enough to state what each individual or group needs to survive on its own turf. In the long run, it is not possible for parts of the world to thrive while others remain desperately poor and deeply frustrated. Further, the world of the future—with its ubiquitous search engines, robots, and other computational devices—will demand capacities that until now have been mere options. To meet this new world on its own terms, we should begin to cultivate these capacities now.[13]

Gardner summarizes the *Five Minds for the Future* with the following terms and their definitions:

The *disciplined mind* has mastered at least one way of thinking—a distinctive mode of cognition that characterizes a specific scholarly discipline, craft, or profession...
The *synthesizing mind* takes information from disparate sources, understands and evaluates that information objectively, and puts it together in ways that make sense...
The *creating mind* breaks new ground. It puts forth new ideas, poses unfamiliar questions, conjures up fresh ways of thinking, and arrives at unexpected answers...
The *respectful mind* notes and welcomes differences between human individuals and between human groups, tries to understand these "others," and seeks to work effectively with them...
The *ethical mind* conceptualizes how workers can serve purposes beyond self-interest and how citizens can work unselfishly to improve the lot ...[14]

As we expand our intellectual capacities, we will also discover that we will become more and more comfortable and proficient in diverse situations. We'll not need to rely on our well-used excuses for standing on the sidelines, but rather, we'll find that we engage more readily as we follow our *Curiosity* into new learning.

Wisdom

Once you have expanded your ways of perceiving and integrated what you know, you'll discover a certain mental calm. This state of unified knowing is engaged then in service to people, profit, and planet. You'll act from information gained through individual, and through collective, ways of knowing, and you'll do so in a manner that is consistent with ethical systems. This ability is grounded in, but not limited by, past experience or history. You'll also anticipate probable future concerns. *Wisdom* is the sum of learning acquired over time and through the heights and depths of your many experiences.

I suppose that's why we often hear references to age along with comments about *Wisdom*. For example, "She's wise beyond her years." Or about an older person, "He just seems so wise."

We seldom hear *Wisdom* used to describe a child or youth. Instead, we associate this mature understanding that stems from a seasoned life with well-earned knowledge of the broadest kind. In addition, *Wisdom* almost always carries with it calmness rather than tension, as well as a joyful balance within all of life's circumstances.

Wisdom is an attribute rarely used to describe leaders unless their insights and behaviors are judicious, mature, and in harmony with their other leadership capabilities.

Furthermore, some suggestion of spirituality is frequently assumed when referring to *Wisdom*. In ancient times, *Wisdom* was viewed as one of the four virtues and was reserved for the gods. It was not something available for mere mortals. Over the centuries, *Wisdom* became associated with the highest forms of knowledge, and it gradually evolved to include the living of a virtuous and beneficial life in practical terms. Here then is the determining point as it relates to your accumulated knowledge—was it acquired for your use alone or does it have shared value?

In our organizations, we usually turn to the Board of Directors or to the executive team for astute guidance. We assume that the best and most universally beneficial guidance in a situation must obviously come from those with the greatest amount of gray hair and of varied experience. And let's face it, some of us are also influenced by power—the power of position or of wealth, or both. It seems that power and wealth are sufficient for too many so-called leaders to consider themselves to be fountains of wisdom. Or is there something else that qualifies?

Yes, there are smarter criteria than power or wealth when looking for guides and leaders who have the capacity of *Wisdom*. What if promotions and recruitment for our most promising leaders included the following measures? A wise leader must...

- Engage creatively and include non-rational processes in decision-making
- Think deeply and grasp complex situations
- Synthesize what is known, not merely condense the information
- Influence people through skillful use of words and deeds
- Commit to the long-term prosperity of people and planet.

As you mature as a leader, you'll rely on your *Intelligence*, your *Capacity for Perception*, to explore and expand all of your other leadership capacities. More than any other leadership capacity, it is your mind that is your primary tool for developing each of your other capacities.

That is why I have included the material on spiritual intelligence in this chapter. *Wisdom,* like spirituality, is inclusive, integrative, and over-arching. It implies the peak of experience and knowledge. In developing your *Intelligence*, *Wisdom* arrives after you attend to your other stages of intellectual development.

Coda

Damien kept his job. In fact he became a vocal advocate for ways the organization could retain some of the studio atmosphere even though they were now growing rapidly. On at least one occasion, he commented to me that he would bet there were lots of other people out there like him who struggled in their school years, university education, and professions just because they processed information so differently from the norm.

And at the end of our coaching relationship in a meeting with Damien and the CEO, the CEO was gracious and complimentary to Damien for all that he did to turn himself around. And then he turned to me and asked me what I had done; he wondered what magic I had used to effect such a change in Damien.

I looked at Damien, and we exchanged a knowing glance. Damien told him about how he'd reconfigured the team meetings and was already working with an interior designer to change the floor plan in their department.

In the weeks following that meeting with the CEO, Damien oversaw the renovations with offices and cubicles surrounding a large open space in the center with casual seating and tables where staff could huddle to work out a challenge or predicament they faced. He hosted a twice-weekly working meeting in which his direct reports discussed their department's projects. He added that what was so surprising was how similar these team meetings were to the lab sessions he had in grad school in which the entire class would engage in an egalitarian exchange of ideas and challenges.

It had been several years since I heard from Damien, then he recently called to give me an update. He said that after a year of his department working in this new way, the CEO asked him to initiate a project for the entire home office so that every other department team and project team would conduct their work with full consideration for the different ways that employees learn and process information.

He was now practicing the art of leadership.

*Do not follow
where the path may lead.
Go instead
where there is no path
and leave a trail.*

–Muriel Strode

7

INITIATIVE
Capacity for Action

Justin

Justin appeared straight from central casting, playing the part of the executive. He wore a tie, pressed slacks, and trimmed-to-perfection salt and pepper hair. Oh, and his shirt had those cool little monogrammed initials on the left cuff. Dapper.

I noticed his accent when he first spoke, a unique lilting quality. If you had asked me, I would have guessed that his first language came from somewhere east of the Adriatic. After that initial observation, I didn't take particular notice of this vocal trait until it came up later in our work together.

Though he looked the part of an executive, he didn't seem to act the part. He was hesitant, in a slow-to-get-started way. He walked as if he were being moved about the room by an unseen force outside himself. If a camera only showed him from the waist up, you would think he intended to go where he was headed. A full-length shot would show something different. He walked like someone who didn't want to leave an impression in the carpet. He walked a bit flat-footed, and his steps seemed tentative.

He was a participant in one of the management skills programs I taught. I assumed from his attire that he held a higher position than the other participants; that was my initial (wrong) impression. As it turned out, his boss was also in the room, a guy wearing a sweater, much more casual in dress.

Justin didn't voluntarily speak up in the three-day training session, although nearly every one of his peers did. He willingly participated in the small group activities, but in no way did he stand out. I easily forgot all about him until several months later when the CEO and Justin's boss, the Vice President of Operations, asked me to take on Justin as a coaching client. Here were two top-level decision makers prepared to invest in Justin. What had I missed on my radar screen when I first met him?

It wasn't until I began my professional relationship with Justin that I began to I recall the physical impressions I mentioned above. Justin and I agreed to meet in the lobby of a large hotel in Atlanta. I arrived early and camped out in a comfortable, yet isolated, corner where I could watch for his arrival and where Justin and I could maintain some privacy. I sent him a text pinpointing my location and sat back to drink my coffee and wait.

I watched as he drove up and exchanged his car for a valet ticket. He arrived on time, but he walked as though he had no destination in mind. Maybe he wasn't as eager for this meeting as I had expected. Maybe coaching was someone else's good idea, and he was simply going along with it.

As I sat across from him, I took in more about him. Justin was no longer a young man. In fact, I learned he was fifty-seven years old. Maybe it was his seasoned appearance that had led me to believe he occupied a higher seat in the organization.

"What do you want to achieve through our coaching relationship?" I asked.

He answered in a measured tone, "I aim to become this company's next CEO."

Well, that wasn't very subtle. He certainly knew what he wanted. Except this career aspiration wasn't the reason his boss and his boss's boss had hired me. They believed that he could continue to perform quite well as Senior Director of Operations if he could accomplish two things: one, act with more urgency and two, communicate openly with those above and below him before simply dropping major business plans on their desks. They had made no mention of his aspiration to become a C-level executive. In fact, both of them seemed content to simply patch up his flaws so the business could continue to survive. Nothing they said hinted at their concern for his professional or personal fulfillment. In fact, both of these leaders seemed focused solely on smooth operations and profitable quarters. They were like a couple of engineers needing to retool a piece of equipment.

So began my journey on this swinging footbridge of Justin's hopes across a ravine filled with his fears. I discovered this ravine was as deep and treacherous as the misunderstandings and undelivered expectations surrounding his career and his personal life. Plus he worked for two people who really didn't have his back. This would be an interesting challenge for me.

I soon learned that his current position wasn't Justin's first rodeo. For ten years, he had been the Controller in another company, and he had worked in several other operational and financial capacities throughout his career. Somehow his CEO ambition didn't match his reality. Yet, I asked him why he had taken his current position.

His aspiration to be a businessman and to be at the top of the organizational food chain went back a long way. When he came to this country as a young man from Hungary and entered university, he had imagined himself as his family's hero. He worked at several jobs while he got his degree, and he was eager for the time when he would be able to support his parents who still lived in Budapest. He was to be the son who went to America and became rich and famous.

Along his life's path, he discovered that he just didn't quite have the get-up-and-go he needed to meet those expectations. He appeared to lack that certain drive I've seen in other people who strive, who sacrifice, or who seem endowed with a natural ability to be at the front of the line.

Then he revealed something that he said he had never told anyone, including his wife. As he spilled his story, it all began to make more sense. He was the one in the household who managed the finances. That made perfect sense since accounting, record keeping, and balance sheets were second nature for him. At some point many years ago, he had borrowed against his home mortgage to invest in a friend's new business. He had been planning to leave his controller job and to become a senior executive in this other business. He was content to tough it out and conceal his dream because his true future lay just within his reach.

Then, the new business opportunity became a new business debacle. Bottom line...he lost his shirt and his dream. Furthermore, he lost his financial security and the parachute he thought he so carefully packed for his leap into the future. His wife assumed that he was just having some tough days at the office as he attempted to maintain the ruse. He didn't want to destroy the life style she enjoyed. For a while now, he had been telling himself, "Hey, once I'm CEO everything will be just fine, and I'll take my wife on a nice vacation to Italy."

He had made some bad choices, and he had kept secrets. And now he imagined that if he could just become CEO, he'd be able to overcome his financial, familial, and psychological fears. To him, CEO meant freedom though he had never done the deep inner work needed to be a leader. He said he was always too busy or too distracted by urgent demands. Now his internal chaos was playing out in his bank account.

There had been enough lies so I told him a painful truth, "I realize that you have an image of becoming a CEO, but I just don't see it."

In my first career, I was a building contractor. I learned a bit about putting things together and what is required to create a solid structure. It's never a good idea to build on a weak foundation. And when you remodel, sometimes you just have to demolish more than you expected and start at the bottom and rebuild correctly. Another coat of paint was not going to fix Justin's situation.

He had to begin by removing the decayed assumptions that he would become his parent's savior. He had to reenter the crawlspace underneath his marriage and replace the pretty, but rotten, bricks with a solid and reinforced foundation of honesty. And he needed to install up-to-date financial operating systems at home with third party auditing, like he had done for his company. Right now, all he had was a huge dumpster full of debris that was on its way to the landfill; there was nothing to recycle here.

Surprisingly, yet critically, the key factor in our work together became his speech. Do you recall I mentioned that when I first met him I had noticed his accent? It turned out that Justin carried a deep embarrassment about the way he thought he sounded to other people. Since English was not his first language, he became very self-conscious when he spoke. Well, there was one reason he was quieter than his peers.

As it turned out, he had spent his adulthood listening very carefully to others, and he had honed a keen perception of what others meant when they spoke. Yet he didn't trust his own voice. He had not developed the necessary awareness of his own volition and of the link that existed between the choices he made and his energy.

Initiative—Capacity for Action

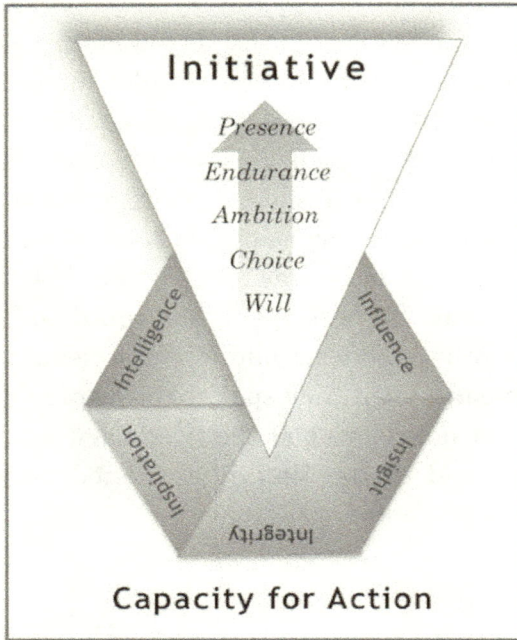

Initiative is your supply of energy, and it fuels the enterprise of your Self. Others often view leaders as individuals who are perpetually driven by an inner force, as though they were the embodiment of energy. Though most of us can muster a *reaction* to what another person says or does, we are not as familiar with our own internal initiating impulse.

Among all the traits we ascribe to leaders, the fact that they "get things done" is probably the single-most agreed upon observation. We're drawn toward those who step forward when the rest of us hesitate and toward those who speak when the rest of us feel tongue-tied. This characteristic to act distinguishes these individuals, so we follow them, and we name them our leaders.

In my early research about what it takes to become a leader, I was fascinated by this unique ability of some individuals to simply act. I wondered, what was the process that differentiates a leader from the rest of us? I wondered how one develops the *Capacity for Action.*

I began to explore what it is that we all have, to one degree or another, which enables each of us to function, and for still others to act when most of us would either hesitate or withdraw. I started with action, with doing, and then worked my way backwards to its source. And here's the process, as I understand it.

As with every other capacity, the five stages of *Initiative* advance from an invisible interior force, and then gradually they become a noticeable exterior expression. At its core, internally, you'll first experience *Initiative* as your *Will,* an impulse that you can sense, though few of us do because of a stronger unconscious and instinctual tendency to simply act. And then after your *Will,* but before you act, you experience *Choice,* an internal and often unconscious selection process that you'll employ to determine possible action. Once you choose, your initiating energy then involves *Ambition,* the actual locus of action. *Initiative* then further develops into the capability to perpetuate, to keep on doing, called *Endurance.* Eventually, *Initiative* becomes its full expression as *Presence.*

Let me explain that *Will,* as well as the next stage, *Choice,* are hard to describe and to differentiate because in our culture we focus so intently on their results, on action. And as you'll see, action actually occurs after you experience both *Will* and *Choice.* Consequently, I need to weave between them and their distinctions as we explore these two stages.

Let's begin your discovery of *Initiative* nearest to your center, your *Will.*

The Will

The *Will* is the fountainhead of volition. *Will* is simply the pure impulse that comes from your center, which might eventually become a word or deed. In addition, it's your *Will* that becomes activated when you hear that inner voice telling you that if anything is going to happen it's up to you.

Will is not to be confused with "willpower," the forceful effort to dominate other psychological processes. In his book, *The Act of Will*, Roberto Assagioli describes *Will* and willpower this way.

> The Victorian conception of the will still prevails, a conception of something stern and forbidding, which condemns and represses most of the other aspects of human nature. But such a misconception might be called a caricature of the will. The true function of the will is not to act against the personality drives to *force* the accomplishment of one's purposes. The will has a *directive* and *regulatory* function; it balances and constructively utilizes all the other activities and energies of the human being without repressing any of them.[1]

Assagioli's description of the *Will* sounds a lot like the maestro you met back in chapter 2. And each of us has also experienced willpower. For example, you just ate a delicious chocolate chip cookie, and you're about to reach for another when you think about the added calories it puts into your system. Or you groan a little from the thought of tomorrow's workout and the number of reps you'll need to do to simply atone for another cookie. And you suppress your desire even though you're already imagining how yummy another one would taste. You exercise your willpower and resist taking another cookie.

It wasn't until the prospect of eating a second or third cookie that you exercised your willpower and you suppressed that chocolaty urge. And that is how most of us think about our *Will*, but the *Will* is something different. It's the initiating volitional spark, not a later occurring limiting force.

The distinction here is that willpower functions in an inhibitory way. It overpowers and subdues. It limits and controls our options. Whereas the *Will* is a deep inner generative experience of the self, of individuality—distinct from another, that ignites the possibility that we act in the direction of our goal.

The *Will* is not a passive force that you only become aware of after you see the effect of your actions. No, it's an always-available dynamism that is too often ignored until you are called upon to act because of a crisis or threat. And if you have not deliberately exercised your *Will* beforehand, then you are apt to suffer from under developed volition, and you could come up lacking in resolve to face your challenge.

This was what happened with Justin. He held onto an image of becoming a CEO, yet he could barely direct his own body to move purposefully across a room, let alone assert himself and his aspirations to his boss. He appeared to be a "nice guy," but no one else could see the CEO picture he carried in his own mind. Fundamentally, Justin was un*will*ing to take the trouble, or to pay the price, to close the gap between his dream and his reality.

Most of the time we associate the words I'm using in this chapter, like initiative, will, ambition, or endurance, with something we "do." For example: we "start" a project, we "volunteer" for a task force, we "work out" twice as long as most people, or we "keep typing" until the document is finished. All these descriptions have something in common; they relate to something physical that we may be doing. However, as you explore your *Capacity for Action*, it's critical that you understand how these *doing* activities originate. Let's dig in a bit deeper.

Many writers and practitioners in the field of Psychosynthesis, first articulated by its founder, Roberto Assagioli, describe the *Will* as having three distinct characteristics:

There is the *strong will*—the physical aspect of the *Will* that is focused on "doing." It indicates power, energy, or force. It manifests, generates, or produces outcomes.

Then there is the *skillful will*—the mental aspect of the *Will* that suggests a planning or strategic ability to achieve desired results by spending the least amount of energy.

And finally there is the *good will*—the emotional aspect of the *Will* such as love, compassion, and empathy that generates connections and ensures the welfare of others, especially the protection of another's *Will*.

If you look at these different ways that your *Will* informs your choices, you see that your *Capacity for Action* can be magnificently fine-tuned to include all types of *Will* at the same time. Then, to deliver on these impulses, you activate each aspect of your personality—your body, your mind, and your heart.

Expanding your *Capacity for Action* by developing your *Will* requires deliberate attention and effort to exercise, similar to when you go to the gym. Few of us work out at the gym solely for the activities that are available there. No, you exercise so that you can increase your ability to achieve something else of greater value than merely lifting the weights or running the laps. Perhaps you want to increase your blood flow or to increase your flexibility, all of which results in a healthier body. In the same way, you probably don't use your bike as your required mode of transportation, but rather as a way to increase your cardiovascular health, to hang out with friends, or to travel slowly, all of which could result in a healthier body and an increase to your longevity.

Similarly, you can "exercise" to develop your *Will*. One way is to engage your physical body in an activity. Because you are expanding your *Capacity for Action,* you can experience this expansion by using your body, which is full of action. Any kind of physical activity, even the forms listed in the previous paragraph, done deliberately and with attention on developing your *Will*, are effective.

Try walking, for example. Practice walking slowly, which requires moving your foot ahead, placing your heel down, rolling your foot forward through your extended toes, and finally lifting that foot up. Repeat with the other foot. By the way, don't do this if you actually want to get somewhere. This type of walking is an exercise in deliberately observing and directing something that has become automatic for you. Try walking by keeping your attention on actually causing each movement in your feet to occur. Notice how deliberately you must act in order to simply walk.

You can also build your *Will* by reading biographies of outstanding individuals or accounts of other's incredible efforts. Read slowly, pausing to highlight sections that grab your attention. In this way, you are activating your *Imagination*. This is why I include heroic literature as required reading for my leadership development programs. It encourages participants to develop a more activated *Will*.

Let's say that you've consciously started activities such as walking meditation or reading about other's feats. Perhaps, you've read about the travails of mountaineers, or you've listened to a classical score with attention to the myriad volitional acts it takes for the composer to produce the piece and the musicians to perform it.

Perhaps, you've read books describing the struggles of other leaders. Notice that you have a smorgasbord of options in front of you. What did you choose? Did you select your *Will* training exercise from the arts, or from music, or sport, politics, social sciences, or literature, or physical science? What draws you, and what pushes you? What happens next is that you encounter *Choice*—the ability to select from options.

Choice

Choice is the normal occurrence that follows the potential thoughts and actions that are generated by your *Will*. A selection and sorting process now occurs. For example, you don't say every word you think (do you?). And you don't perform every activity that you think about. Somewhere between initiation and action there is an editing process—you choose.

Imagine that we're sitting in a cafe. You're describing a decision that you made at work this week. Pause a moment before you read on and actually recall a decision you made this past week...Pause.

Now I'll ask you why you made the decision that you did...Pause.

And I bet you quickly came up with a reason for your decision. You might say that you decided to do X because it was what the customer really needed, or because it was the right thing to do, or because you felt there were no other options.

Regardless of your answer to my "why" question, consider for a moment that you chose; you made a choice, you selected an option. For a moment, try to let go of the story about your choice and simply notice that you chose.

This is also when you might feel like you need to defend a decision. You might even claim that you were simply exercising your "free will." It's as if you're seeking to protect choosing as a right that is granted to you, somewhat like air.

Okay, this is what I was trying to help you see; we are so often wrapped up in the content of our choices that we seldom notice that we actually possess this marvelous capability to choose.

A leader who is reluctant to choose, or who delays choosing, or who is unable to choose may be either immobilized by fear or caught in a series of circumstances already chosen by others. Or, a leader could be acting impulsively without being aware of the role that *Choice* plays in the development of *Initiative*. The moment many people first realize that they have actually made a choice is when its consequences show up and the outcome of their choice isn't at all what they expected. So remember, "not choosing" when faced with options is also a choice.

Now, let's look more deeply at your ability to choose in its purest form. The kind of choosing I'm talking about here is "choosing to choose." In his book *Essentialism*, leadership and business consultant Greg McKeown writes.

> For too long, we have overemphasized the external aspect of choices (our options) and underemphasized our internal ability to choose (our actions). This is more than semantics. Think about it this way. Options (things) can be taken away, but our core ability to choose (free will) cannot be.

> We need to recognize [our ability to choose] as an invincible power within us, existing separate and distinct from any other thing, person, or force. William James once wrote, 'My first act of free will shall be to believe in free will.' That is why the first and most crucial skill you can learn on this journey is to develop your ability to choose choice, in every area of your life.[2]

Many purported leaders have adopted the prevalent practice of "learned helplessness." They have relinquished their agency, their responsibility to make choices for themselves. Justin was well practiced at this. He was waiting for someone or some other circumstance to appear before he thought he could act. If you waive your right and your responsibility to choose like Justin, then you cannot marshal the energy to act, to continue an endeavor like a team project, a corporate initiative, or a creative solution to a common need.

Victor Frankl, a Holocaust survivor and author of the book *Man's Search for Meaning*, wrote, "Everything can be taken from a man but one thing: the last of the human freedoms—to choose one's attitude in any given set of circumstances, to choose one's own way."[3]

I have to believe that Frankl, who was unjustly accused and who faced a Nazi death camp, knows something very fundamental about *Choice*. He consciously chose to stay alive as long as he lived, to find some source of beauty everyday, to perform mental exercises to stay alert, while many others in his circumstances unconsciously chose to relinquish their agency. *Choice* is something that cannot be taken from you without your permission.

Reading this material about choosing in the face of severe situations like Frankl faced might seem irrelevant. Yet some form of deliberation always precedes conscious choosing; and choosing means that you prefer one thing, one action, or even one method to another. As a leader, you will need to make many choices, and some of your decisions will, no doubt, burden you more than others. Perhaps, the most potentially crippling situation you'll face as a new leader is when you realize that to choose will force you to discard other quite reasonable options.

However, your courage to do so will strengthen an internal muscle and lead to an even greater level of confidence in, and appreciation for, your *Capacity for Action* versus inaction. Your ability to make the tough calls, especially as it shows up in decision-making, is your central responsibility, and it obviously involves choosing.

Our discussion would not be complete without returning to the notion of willpower, which I mentioned earlier. While many psychologists and philosophers have identified the *Will* as the center of human energy, few have followed it to its source like social psychologist and professor, Roy Baumeister.

In their book *Willpower*, Baumeister and his colleagues have looked at three major functions of the brain: self-control, choosing, and decision-making. They discovered that the three share a common resource. Through recent studies in the lab, they've discovered some interesting links between brain function and food.

In order for your brain to function well, you need massive amounts of glucose, which is delivered via the bloodstream from the various foods you eat. Once in your brain, glucose converts to neurotransmitters—the chemicals that brain cells use to send signals. Now here's the surprise. This supply of energy is finite.

Baumeister and his team discovered that the fuel that drives decision-making (choosing) and self-control (willpower) come from the same tank. And they concluded that there is a direct correlation between self-control and nutrition. Consider, for a moment, how most leaders you know go about their day. They grab a bagel and coffee on the way to the office, meet with a team over lunch while they're served catered sandwiches, chips, and soda, and then they grab their dinner at the end of the day. I really wonder what effect balanced nutrition, at the first part of one's day, would have on the quality of a leader's decision-making throughout the day.

In addition, since both of the brain functions come from the same tank of fuel, if you've been exercising self-control (willpower), you have less fuel to energize your decision-making. Hmm, I wonder if that could be why some leaders we depend on to make lots of decisions every day and who exercise self-control over their diets, their appearance, or their thoughts, lose it all and act like unleashed adolescents from time to time. Might this explain some of the indiscretions of morals, ethics, and decency that we've seen from many leaders in high places?

Baumeister says he coined the term "ego-depletion," "...for describing people's diminished capacity to regulate their thoughts, feelings, and actions. People can sometimes overcome mental fatigue, but [he] found that if they had used up energy by exerting willpower (or by making decisions...) they would eventually succumb."[4]

These findings point to the need for you, as an Inside*OUT* leader, to exercise nutritional self-care and to manage both how many cookies you eat and how your fuel supply is used. You must first wisely choose how to spend your resources before you attempt to undertake the massive responsibilities required to guide and deploy your organization's resources.

As you can see throughout this section and others, expanding your capacities is not achieved in a linear fashion. There is an inter-relationship across all your capacities. To make wise *Choices*, you will also need to rely on your other capacities of *Intelligence, Integrity*, and your level of *Insight*. Your ability to choose includes your ability to differentiate. When you instruct your followers to look here, and not there, you have already made a differentiating choice and are now communicating that to your team.

Now, all this internal work you've been doing on your stages of *Will* and *Choice* is about to become visible to the rest of us on the outside. How well you're developing your *Capacity for Action* is about to be on display.

Ambition

Ambition is the productive energy you experience that flows from the selections you make through disciplined and conscious choosing. You now need to make withdrawals from your *Will* and *Choice* accounts in order to have enough energy to act. Your amount of fuel will depend on how much you invested in developing these first two stages. When you deliberately develop your *Initiative*, you avail yourself of a free supply of energy. Let me explain this through a couple of stories.

One of my clients, who had been an executive with a pharmaceutical company, tapped into this free supply of energy after a near-fatal accident. First some background. His company noticed very early in his career that he was someone to be groomed for leadership. He possessed solid technical skills as well as the relational qualities needed to reach one of their goals: expanding treatment options in human health care. He was definitely a rising star.

Then while out cycling on an early morning workout, a motorist crossed the road and hit this rising star head-on. He was seriously injured but fortunately got the highly experienced and rapid medical attention he so desperately needed. Experts attended to his shattered bones and to his mangled muscles and arteries. Mercifully, he had not suffered a head injury. Then, several weeks into his recovery, he realized that his head wasn't as fine as everyone had first assumed.

After enduring six weeks of surgeries and physical therapy, here's how Michael O'Brien explains his experience in his memoir, *Shift*.

> Even though I thought I was doing my best to stay positive, I had to admit, I wasn't showing up with a 100% positive attitude....In private, I was bitter and angry. I felt like a burden. I also realized that I probably wasn't fooling anybody....In that moment, I made a commitment to myself that the next day would be a new start....If I was going to be the best husband, father, and person I could be, I had to stop thinking of 'best' in comparison to other people or as an unattainable idea I had in my head. In order to do this, I had to shift from the perspective of a victim to that of a victor. This wasn't the life that I had planned for myself and my family, but it was an opportunity to be defined, not by what had happened to me, but by how I responded to it. The drive and desire to get better couldn't come from outside of myself: it had to come from the inside.[5]

His life did change because he changed it. As he unleashed the flow of energy available to him, his body healed though not without ongoing complications. And his *Ambition,* which resulted from his choice to choose and to thereby change his attitude, eventually empowered him to also change his career. He now coaches and guides other leaders to tap into the free supply of energy that flows from aligning their *Ambition* with wise choices.

Yet, not all wake-up alarms result in an awakening. Some people become irritated, feel wronged, or choose to ignore the impact of their choices. After all, memory foam and down comforters have a way of appealing to inertia like little else.

Except there's nothing quite like a head-on collision with an SUV, or with some other life altering experience, to force you to make a choice about your attitude and perspective. It gives you time to reexamine your trajectory and consider whether it's the result of your choices or someone else's. The jolt you can experience to your complacency is the infusion of energy that is often needed to propel you onward on your life's intended path. This is why I started our exploration of the Inside*OUT* leader with *Identity*. I wanted you to examine why you're here and where you're going relative to your mission.

Here's a contrasting example. I had another client who always fretted about the all-too-long winter weather where he lived in the U.S. because it was unpleasant and oft times impossible for him to get outdoors and enjoy his favorite sport—fly-fishing. His employer offered him a promotion and a salary increase to oversee the operations at their largest manufacturing facility if he would relocate. He chose to accept. This seemed like a sensible career move.

Except, the relocation required a move to a Canadian prairie city. Now he was living out someone else's most expedient solution to a company need. And in the move, he lost touch with the activity that really nourished him—fly-fishing. Of course, you and I both know that he could have taken a temporary vacation from his sport or he might have chosen to fall in love with hockey or ice fishing. But no, he chose to grieve about the situation. He felt depressed, blamed the company, and who knows, he might also have been experiencing seasonal affective disorder. In any case, he was suffering.

Here was an individual who had lost his *Capacity for Action,* as well as his dream, because of competing choices. He allowed himself to become trapped by the image of what being a Vice-President in his organization would mean to him. He had an opportunity, but he lost his energy. He did not choose to align with what fueled his spirit, or stirred his *Will,* or informed his *Choice.* Accordingly, he didn't receive the energy from *Ambition* that he might have.

Ambition means that something has been birthed, and *Initiative* includes responsibility for its outcomes. Leaders who are impotent don't originate, nor do they generate. In fact, they become the fodder of others' choices and objectives. Our fly-fishing executive was one of these persons. His supervisor thought he'd be a great asset to the Canadian facility. His move was intended to be a plus for everyone, but what about his overall effectiveness? He wasn't fly-fishing, and since he felt trapped by the climate and his regret about the move, he wasn't leading his organization efficiently. He never chose to make the move his *choice,* and that cost him any energy that would have been available from *Ambition.*

However, you need to be cautious with *Ambition.* Allow me to illustrate. In science, we have two major types of energy: potential and kinetic. Potential energy is energy that is stored but available to be used. On the other hand, kinetic energy is the energy of an object already in motion. Potential energy is waiting for conditions to change so it can become kinetic energy.

Similarly, the energy of *Ambition* is potentially available. But you can only use it once it becomes kinetic, the energy you use when you're moving with your life's purpose.

Your *Ambition* is not simply "available." It's dynamic. Remember how *Initiative* begins with a *Choice* based on *Will?* Therefore, your *Capacity for Action* implies that something is already in motion within you. When you perpetuate this generative force, it expands into the next stage, *Endurance*, that which keeps on keeping on. And herein lies the difference between the cyclist and the fisherman.

Michael, the recovering bicyclist, chose an attitude that aligned with his intention to heal, and he consequently generated the energy to actually heal faster and with greater positive impact than other patients surrounding him. He has become an example of a person embodying kinetic energy. While the angler became frozen by his choice and remained locked in a state of potential: available but immobile. Stuck in mood, job, and place.

What then is the state of your *Ambition*? Are you energized? Are you available for deployment? Are you making choices that sustainably source the way you are leading? Remember that *Ambition* is so much more than intent and desire. It actually creates and generates. It's kinetic.

And in order for you to sustain your leadership, you also need to develop the conditions and stamina necessary to keep it going.

Endurance

Back in chapter 3, I described some of the challenges that Sir Ernest Shackleton faced in the unexpected circumstances he and his men faced. It's also fascinating to consider how the name of his ship foreshadowed both his Antarctic ordeals and the quality of his leading. Though his ship was crushed by the ice and sank, sailors will attest that its spirit remained. And when his vessel, named *"Endurance,"* was christened in 1912, no one could have foreseen the significance of its name.

If you only experience your *Will* as a kind of sporadic firing of your volition, then this stage of *Endurance* will be a vital next step for you in expanding your *Initiative*, your *Capacity for Action. Endurance* is your ability to maintain a steady level of activity, especially when you need to carry on after others have complained about their circumstance or have already given up. Others will perceive your steady power as one of your strengths and admire your continued drive since they themselves might be less familiar with the notion of persistence.

Lessons learned on the marathon course, in the grinding agony of learning to walk again after an accident, or in the face of blatant prejudices against your race, gender, or whom you love are also the lessons of determination that are needed by leaders in the workplace. Perseverance to the very end brings with it a humility that tempers the bravado expressed by those who have not persisted but merely participated.

Many business leaders become so absorbed in the competitive energy of their industry that they loose sight of the application of *Endurance*. As Bill George, former CEO at Medronic, writes in his book *Authentic Leadership*, "Authentic leaders know that competing requires a consistently high level of self-discipline to be successful. Being very competitive is not a bad thing; it is an essential quality of successful leaders, but it needs to be channeled through purpose and discipline."[6]

It is during the stage of *Endurance* when leaders either gracefully mature or act like brats. They either take a stand, or they mock those who do. They either engage in the camaraderie of courteous competition, or they behave like bullies. Those who endure in order to mature become the men and women we want to follow.

Managing your *Endurance* can be a tricky proposition, especially for someone with position and power. The perseverance required for you to endure can easily mutate into its nasty cousin, stubbornness, if you don't integrate it with your other capacities. It's really up to you. Will you focus this incredible energy that is unleashed through your *Initiative*, or will you succumb to your own un*will*ingness to step up to your leadership responsibilities?

In his book, *True Grit*, adventurer Bear Grylls recounts his favorite stories of human effort. Reading heroic tales can be immensely entertaining, but I recommend that leaders might read them in order to consciously expand their own capacities. Then, when called upon to act heroically, you have some idea of how others have done it.

Maybe you had some similar stories read to you as a child. Or you read these types of stories yourself. Maybe you've watch TV shows like *American Ninja Warrior* or *Alone*. Perhaps you even participated in an Ironman, an Ultra long distance race, Tough Mudder, or Spartan competition. Why have these shows and events become so popular? Why do so many folks dream about, train for, and engage in these rigorous physical challenges?

I have a hunch it speaks to our universal human longing to stretch, to expand, to learn, and to overcome. What if you formed a cohort of leaders to undertake a similar approach to developing capacities for leading? What if you devised a rigorous protocol to stretch your relational muscles? What if you learned how, and then actually excelled at, leading? Consider in what ways you would need to endure in order to create and write your own heroic story. What would it take? What could be your next step?

As you embark on this valiant journey of expanding your *Initiative*, you'll experience some parallels to what you discovered in the chapter on *Inspiration*. Here's when you'll discover if you can actually inspire yourself. You'll find out if you can act with the energy that you generate from your own volition and through the choices you make. And you'll discover what many leaders have discovered before you—you don't act because others see you as the leader, you act because you must see yourself as the leader.

Endurance demands that you don't give up—even if you need to adjust your expectations of the outcome. You might choose to persevere like the English naturalist and biologist Charles Darwin, who finally completed his monumental *On the Origin of Species* when his physical energy was so low that he could only work an hour a day. Or perhaps your willingness to endure will be like that of Thomas Edison who said, "I have not failed a thousand times; I've discovered one thousand ways to *not* make a light bulb." Or perhaps you too will assert your determination as the Shackleton family has done through their motto, *"Fortitudine vincimus"* (By endurance we conquer).

And if your ship sinks beneath you, how will you find the energy to carry on?

Presence

Presence is simply being fully here, now; and being nowhere else. When your *Initiative* is fully developed, you are able to be fully at hand physically, mentally, emotionally, and spiritually. *Presence* can't be faked because, at some level, stakeholders will always be aware of its opposite, a leader's absence—the inability to show up. *Presence* is the result of sustained energy arising from a disciplined *Will*.

As you craft this stage of *Presence*, over time you'll also need to draw on your other leadership capacities in order to build and maintain the just and noble endeavor of your growth. At this stage, *Endurance* reaches its full capacity and you'll be living your life on purpose and in the direction of your vision.

I've met a few individuals who embodied *Presence*. Let me tell you about Walter. Here's what I noticed *in me* while I was in Walter's company. When I spoke, I felt totally heard by him. He would simply turn from whatever he was doing or thinking, and he would face me directly. I saw, "Go on," in his sparkling eyes. It was so clear that he was there to serve my agenda and not his.

It's rare to have another person face you squarely and look directly at you.   Given so much of our workspace architecture, team members seldom look directly at you without interrupting themselves to glance at a screen that's lurking in their peripheral vision or to take their eyes off of you to look slightly over your shoulder at someone walking by their office. Walter's focus on me was not because he had been assigned by someone else to be my designated mentor or because of any other external directive. No, he was simply being present to me, to the moment, because he believed that this younger me was worthy of his attention: something very unusual for a seasoned CEO.

Anna also worked in this same company. Along with Walter, she also made a lasting impression on me early in my career. She had been a senior executive in the organization since it's beginning. At first glance, she seemed to have been a graduate of the Margaret Thatcher "iron lady" leadership academy. She carried herself with an elegant, yet accessible, humility that made it easy for each of us junior executives to interact with her. I felt like she was one of us.

Yet, when a junior executive made a mistake that had significant fallout, she was very direct, and her resolve was never masked. She could simultaneously communicate her anger and focus on a resolution. She always maintained her compassion for the organization and for all those impacted by the error, including the one who screwed up. This was the first time I witnessed someone who displayed equal parts of drive and tenderness at the same time.

This synthesis of will and love in a leader's style is what I'm calling *Presence.* It requires you to have an abundant, and readily available, reserve of both of these valuable resources and to exercise wisdom in determining how to deploy this unique blend. When you are able to support and nourish your followers while also providing firm direction, you're both *creating* the process and *trusting in* the process. It means you have the capacity to use your intellect *and* your heart, your receptivity *and* your action. You must be able to take in while you are giving out. You aren't holding your breath and waiting for someone else to make the first move.

You're able to breathe, in and out, and you're able to do this with equal measures of grace and grit.

In his best-selling book, *Good to Great*, Jim Collins points toward *Presence* in his description of the Level 5 Executive. Though he doesn't use the word *presence*, he describes the good-to-great leader as someone with compelling modesty and with unwavering resolve. Here's how he described these qualities in the executives he interviewed during his research.

> They'd talk about the company and the contributions of other executives as long as we'd like but would deflect discussion about their own contributions. When pressed to talk about themselves, they'd say things like, 'I hope I'm not sounding like a big shot.' Or, 'There are plenty of people in this company who could do my job better than I do.'...[And] It is very important to grasp that Level 5 leadership is not just about humility and modesty. It is equally about ferocious resolve, an almost stoic determination to do whatever needs to be done to make the company great.[7]

The concept of *Presence* is a bit obscure and difficult to describe, even though that is precisely what I'm attempting to do in this section. And it's even more difficult to achieve. In fact, I suspect that you cannot attain it, but rather it is something that is granted, or bestowed, upon you once you have developed a certain level of equanimity. It's similar to an honor granted by a monarch or a blessing given to you by another person.

Don't underestimate your role here. There are definitely things you can do and attitudes you can convey that would likely add to your capacity of *Presence*. As with each of the capacities and stages of an Inside*OUT* leader, you don't work towards achieving this fifth stage. You work, and then you receive the acknowledgement.

In their book titled *Presence*, Peter Senge and his colleagues, Scharmer, Jaworski, and Flowers, propose a theory for a deeper level of human learning. They describe a three-phase cyclical process for learning that involves:

1. Sensing; A lot of observing—becoming one with the world
2. Presencing; Retreating and reflecting—allowing an inner knowledge to emerge
3. Realizing; Acting swiftly with a natural flow.

Then, as with all cycles, the process returns to the first phase. This time the cycle contains new information that gets incorporated into the process.

They say that *presencing* is that interval of time during which you're transforming your self and your will. This phase is sandwiched between the previous interval, *sensing*, during which you were transforming your perceptions and immediately prior to another interval, *realizing*, when you will transform your action. So being in the present implies that you just made a huge adjustment to the way you see things (perception) and before you make an equally huge adjustment to the way you usually react. The moment that the authors label presencing is like a kind of pregnant pause, an interval in time that carries immense possibility.

Scharmer explained the rare moment in this way. "To me, presencing is about 'pre-sensing' and bringing into presence—and into the present—your highest future potential. It's not just 'the future' in some abstract sense but my own highest future possibility as a human being."[8]

Senge and his colleagues are describing a process that is deeply psychological and perhaps even abstract. In order to grasp the concept, I imagine that presencing is similar to this more tangible example. I did some mountaineering when I was younger. I read a lot of material, received some instruction, and watched others at their craft. Yet, on my first day on a rope, right before I rappelled down the rock face, all of my hard wiring shouted in my brain that this was dangerous. I was terrified. Yet, I proceeded to triple check all my knots and gear before I slowly crept toward the lip of the precipice. And then, there was that moment when my perception shifted from fear to something like resolve and anticipation for the upcoming act of stepping over the edge.

The key here is that I intentionally moved toward the future without a clear notion of how it would turn out. Immediately prior to feeling my entire weight shift from my feet to the rope, it seemed as if anything could happen. I was "airborne" and my future was full of possibility; I was present. This pivotal moment, immediately prior to my descent, shifted how I would approach all future mountaineering outings as well as other future scary endeavors.

It's in this way that living in the present becomes a recurring openness to possibilities that occur between the moment when we see things differently and when we act upon that insight. *Presence* enables you to hold the apparent contradictory dual experiences of surrender and determination in a way that supplies you with a fierce calm.

As you leave this capacity and explore the next capacity, *Influence*, you're about to discover how your newly expanded *Capacity for Action* provides the energy for you to touch the lives of those on your team and in your community. Remember though to stay humble and tough.

Coda

In this critical leadership capacity, *Insight*, you've seen the necessity of pursuing an integrated development among all your leadership capacities.

Consider that *Insight* without *Initiative* distills to mere information; *Integrity* without *Initiative* becomes self-righteousness; *Inspiration* without *Initiative* results in hallucination; *Intelligence* without *Initiative* turns out to be eccentric; and *Influence* without *Initiative* is impotent. *Initiative* is your fuel source for leading.

What happened to Justin? I spoke to him just a few months ago. He didn't become a CEO. To his credit, during a recent reorganization, he was assigned more responsibilities, and he now leads an even larger team.

But during his accounting of his professional advances, he paused to say that he and his wife employed the guidance of a counselor to support them during the months of reconnecting with truth. They now partnered in decisions about their family finances. His relationship with his wife was now on solid ground and both of them had committed to communicating openly about their previously hidden assumptions about their roles, wants, and needs.

When he picked up the story again about his work, he said that he was disappointed that his new workload hadn't included a promotion or a salary increase, and he wondered if the reason was his all-too-habitual humility, was he just not fierce enough? He sounded gracious and strong. Since I last worked with him, he had made tremendous progress in his efforts to overcome some of his obstacles. For one thing, he began feeling much better about himself. I could hear it in his voice on the phone. He had a certainty that was missing when I first sat with him in that hotel lobby several years earlier.

He knew he needed to become more visible for all the right reasons. So he sought out opportunities to make presentations. He initiated meetings with leaders of other departments and divisions, and he invited them to work with him in creating growth strategies for the organization. Previously, others saw him as the smiling quiet guy who wore monogrammed initials on the cuff of his shirts. Now, his newly found energy and well-crafted presentation skills caused them to sit up and take notice.

Justin transformed once he found his voice. His words became his method for expression and experience, much like a musician uses her violin. His use of language and his accent flowed in unbroken symmetry, and he became a voice to be heard in his company.

He had also begun to read and then to write poetry. Justin had certainly uncovered what he was really looking for most of his life, and he no longer moved about at the whim of others and of fate. He had anchored himself firmly into his very own source of energy and was ready for his most critical audit...the truth about himself.

Though he didn't ascend the corporate ladder in the way he had hoped, he did transform himself. He accepted his career fate with dignity and with strength. And in my mind, he was poised on the edge of new possibilities for how he would live out his career and his relationships. Justin had certainly expanded his *Capacity for Action.*

Several months after my work with Justin ended, I received an email from his boss and the CEO. They were delighted with his transformation, yet they wished that he would've changed much earlier in his career since he just didn't have that many years left to mature into CEO material. He didn't get a career "do over," but he was committed to finish out his career with newly found vigor and purpose.

*Go confidently
in the direction of your dreams.
Live the life
you have imagined.*

—Henry David Thoreau

8

INFLUENCE
Capacity for
Replication

Lars

He entered the room like a breeze. I could almost hear the faint notes of the old ballad, *They Call the Wind Mariah*. Though this movement was all masculine, there was more than mere "blowing in" about his entrance. A field of energy swirled around him. It was a bit like standing near a mini whirlwind that forms in the dusty flats of America's West. Oh, there was nothing threatening about him at all, quite the opposite, his entrance was even somewhat mesmerizing. He smiled readily, and his laughter filled the room.

Others seemed to know what to expect, but I had never met Lars. Nor had his supervisor alerted me to this energetic individual when she briefed me about her team. We had gathered for an executive team building retreat and their annual strategic planning session. I was to facilitate the meeting.

These gatherings often have a bit of "best-in-show" quality about them. A room full of egos leaves little air for an outsider to breathe. I immediately noticed something different about Lars. It was his oomph. It was big, yet unpretentious. There was an everyone-turns-in-his-direction magnetism that had already captured his peers, and now, I too was about to be brought into his vortex.

He had dark hair and bright blue eyes. Wow, his merriment wasn't only charming, his eyes seemed to laugh out loud as well. His stance was erect, and he walked as though he knew where he was going. Here was a man on a mission, and I was eager to discover a lot more about him. I wanted to know where he was headed.

A few weeks after the meeting, my client, the Vice-President of Marketing and Lars's supervisor, asked if I would coach Lars. I jumped at the opportunity. This launched the beginning of a long and ever-closer working relationship between Lars and me.

I discovered that he was actually a bit older than his youthful appearance and that he had already served in field sales and corporate human resources. He was now in his second position within the marketing group. Each of his previous supervisors saw huge potential in him and made it possible for him to acquire a multidisciplinary approach to the business.

Here was a highflier, already accustomed to the path of speedy and solid career advancement. Delightfully, he lacked the arrogance so often seen in the corporate jocks. He seemed genuine and at ease with others. What could I have to offer him that he didn't already possess as part of his native aptitude?

During our first phase of coaching, he revealed something very personal that he thought had helped to shape his bearing. His mother had spent most of her adult life in and out of psychiatric facilities. He had been estranged from his dad since he was fifteen. His older brother died while fighting in Iraq, and his siblings' lives reflected the complications of drug abuse. His younger brother and sister depended upon Lars for guidance and financial help. His wife and children relied on him as well.

Here was a person who had sufficient reasons to blame his parents for any difficulties he faced. I have worked with many people who struggle to author their own lives, but Lars was not one of them. He was the rare individual who didn't even blink in the face of a challenge. He seemed to become even more fully alert when faced with a formidable situation.

He had risen within each of his assigned departments. On some assignments, he would be tasked with a special project. He'd create a strategic plan, assemble a team, and manage that project team to a timely conclusion. His most useful skills lay in the areas of working with people up and down the organization, and those skills hadn't gone unnoticed.

Eventually, he graduated from departments to business units. Just when he might have taken on the leadership of the

U.S. Marketing Group, he accepted an offer to be country chief in one of the European markets. In this way, his corporate guides provided him yet another huge growth opportunity to manage the business and its people in an overseas location. And Lars knew to grab it.

He was soon applying himself outside of his previously familiar disciplines, and he was supervising executives who had all the needed subject matter expertise, knowledge, and experience that was new to Lars. He was also negotiating with in-country governmental affairs that impacted his company's presence and profitability.

I worked with Lars and with his various executive teams in the U.S. and overseas for nearly 10 years, and during the entire time, I always felt like he was taking me to a higher level in my own growth as a professional. It wasn't always comfortable for me. His preferences for how he wanted me to work with his teams and even his curiosity and commitment to his own excellence pushed me to greater humility, vulnerability, and eventual evolution. And he paid *me* for my opportunity to grow. What an arrangement!

Early on in our coaching relationship Lars faced the common challenge to "just do it" himself. He was so good at what he did that he became impatient with bringing others up-to-speed on a task.

Another of his early challenges was communicating his desires to his staff in a clear and instructive manner. His impatience caused him to do more of the speaking in an interaction. He had given little thought to listening for how his directions were being absorbed. He was well liked, but some of his team members told me that they wished he provided more guidance. Because he was more of a "sender" than a "receiver," he was missing some of the more subtle hints his staff members were sending his way.

Over the course of my work with Lars, I observed how quickly he would move from becoming aware of a flaw, to accepting it, to overcoming his challenge. He had no obvious defensive reaction to feedback. He examined the problem, worked to correct it, and established a new and better habit. Within a few months, he was able to see weaknesses in others that were similar to his own and was asking me how he could help them as well. He was willing to be personally vulnerable about his own struggles, and he was insightful and compassionate while developing his team members. He wanted to leverage his own learnings for the benefit of those around him. Lars's eagerness to move from being my protégé to mentoring his own people was one of his enduring and endearing qualities.

With each new assignment in his career journey, Lars contracted with me to design and facilitate team-building sessions. Most of the sessions would then result in multiple follow-on all-team skill building sessions in which he co-facilitated with me as we taught and coached his team. In these sessions, the team tackled real-world business issues while employing their newly learned skills and processes.

Here was Lars pouring himself not only into the mission of his company but also into the lives of his staff. He was not only executing the business goals of the parent company, he was also curating a most treasured resource—the organization's future leaders. He was shaping those around him.

What was he actually doing? What leadership capacity did he embody?

Influence—Capacity For Replication

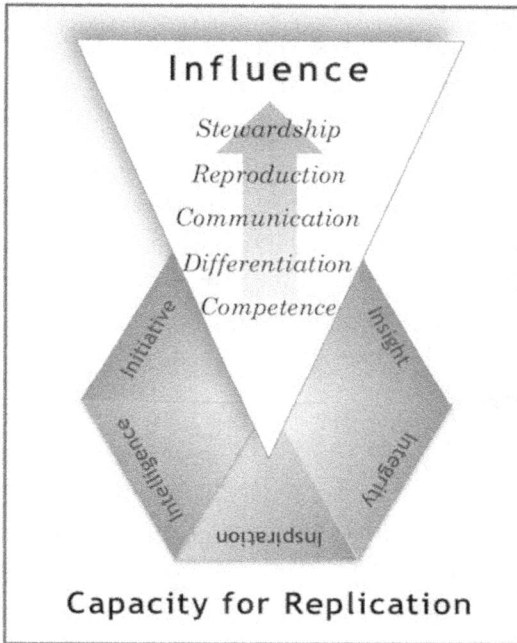

Influence is the capacity for replicating yourself. It assures a succession of leaders within your organization. This capacity is needed if you're going to enroll others in your vision and perpetuate that vision. It's also vital in the progression of your professional development from individual contributor, to a mover of people, to a maker of leaders.

Unlike the vital, though passive, function of the deck prism on the old sailing ship that made possible better living conditions, your capacity of *Influence* is an active, engaging, and deliberate set of behaviors and strategies in order to effect positive change.

Many leaders struggle in their emerging role as leaders. They've become comfortable doing the work themselves, and they now find it challenging to simply guide the dedicated efforts of others.

Unlike a micro-manager, as an Inside*OUT* leader, you have the capacity to touch, move, and inspire others to join an effort and to willingly contribute their best. Expanding your capacity for *Influence* starts deep inside yourself as you experience your own individual *Competence,* and then you develop *Differentiation,* a keen sense of what is really important. Your development radiates outward as skillful *Communication* that reflects your maturity. Then through *Reproduction,* you become a coach and guide for those who also want to lead. Eventually you're practicing *Stewardship* of resources at all levels in the organization.

Competence

At this stage in the progression of your *Capacity for Replication,* you're skillful because you possess a refined ability in some area that pertains to the work at hand. Your knack for *Influence* begins when you have confidence in your ability to lead an endeavor because of your subject matter expertise, your technical skill, or your relational proficiency. As a competent leader, you are not only skillful in some area of unique ability, but you also know that your ability is exemplary, causing other people to notice and to willingly align with your vision and direction.

Lars was not only competent in his assigned tasks and projects, he could also employ his relational intelligence with the people around him, which showed up in that energetic magnetism I saw when I first met him.

Some so-called-leaders appear to rely exclusively on a kind of compulsory influence using their power or their position to sway others. Their leadership capacities have not yet developed in the balanced way that I've discussed in other chapters. Instead, they act on the impulses of one of their subpersonalities that is seeking fulfillment of some unmet primal need. These under-developed leaders frequently gain the spotlight by their behaviors. And since many journalistic organizations are driven by a if-it-bleeds-it-leads editorial approach, we hear about way too many of these leaders in business, government, or religion acting like little girls and boys playing at an adult job with awesomely powerful toys. These individuals gleefully display their hubris—and incompetence—because they believe that others are favorably influenced by their antics.

However, the people we most admire nearly always do at least one thing very well. Think about someone you admire. What specifically does this person do that you find remarkable? If you cannot name their area of proficiency, then you might simply be star-struck.

I recall a person who influenced me early in my life. As a youth, my world didn't include people who were especially eloquent. Though many of these people favorably influenced my values and beliefs, most were not educated or skillful in grammar and vocabulary. Then one semester when I was in college, I was invited to hear a speech by the president of the graduate school. I cannot recall his name or his topic, but I can still hear his delivery. One of my professors had tipped us off beforehand, and so I was prepared to listen for the music in his delivery. I recall thinking at the time that the rhythm and impact of his speech was not unlike a well-played Mozart symphony. And because I wanted to become someone who would use speech to inform and persuade, I was respectfully impressed.

Most of us can recall others who have affected us, but we seldom attend to the cultivation of our own purposeful impact on others. What skills are you developing or refining so that you are certain of becoming exemplary? Are you able to humbly, yet unequivocally, claim a unique aptitude? If yes, then what specifically can you claim as your *Competence*? If no, when will you begin your craft?

If you think that it's too late for you to acquire a unique aptitude, rest assured, there's still time for you to become remarkable. Here are a few options. In the *Talent Code,*

Daniel Coyle says that you can likely become expert at something by investing approximately 10,000 hours of practice. That sounds like a huge chunk of time. In fact, it's approximately five years of a full-time job.

Is he saying that you must really eat, sleep, and drink your dream? Well, yes. And no. He supports his premise by providing many examples of individuals who have mastered specific skills in this way.

You aren't likely to become competent in the first year after you start to play the piano. And you're not likely to become the next Mia Hamm, Leonardo DiCaprio, or Rachel Maddow by dabbling at a hobby. *Competence* requires your commitment over time before you will be perceived as an expert. And it's not merely time investment; it's how you use that time. Many performance experts, including Mr. Coyle himself, now agree that the *alert energy* of the performer, the *targeted focus* of the skill drill, and the *intensity* of the practice are even more critical than merely the accumulation of hours in building *Competence*.

After reading this, do you still want to get really good at leading? Yes? Then it means that you need to get plenty of rest and eat the right foods so you have *alert energy*. Next, select a specific leadership skill and get feedback from others and from video to critique your *targeted* actions. And lastly, do that skill repeatedly and *intensely,* fine-tuning improvements over time. And here's a side benefit: this can even make your work fun.

Your current and future followers are waiting for you to become one of their influencers. It's up to you. The world, or at least your team, is eager to hear your inspiring words that are backed up by your skillful moves. What will be your next step toward becoming the kind of influence among your peers and followers that you've always imagined you could be?

Now that you're focused on becoming competent at something, you are well on your way to the next stage.

Differentiation

This is the ability to define what is important and what is not. *Differentiation* means that you focus your attention and articulate to yourself that which is relevant for your consideration out of all the other shiny objects. Without this ability, you remain uncertain, vacillating in direction, and easily influenced by changing circumstances.

Differentiation is the result of all those focused hours you spent developing your *Competence*. You now have the ability to identify what is pertinent to an endeavor. In his book, *The Art of Leadership,* former CEO Max Depree writes, "The first task of a leader is to define reality."[1]

This ability is so needed in our organizations. People are often longing for their leaders to clearly focus on what they deem vital to the organization's mission. And individuals need to hear this message repeatedly from their leaders.

The problem I often see lies in a leader's unchecked focus. These leaders identify a goal and talk about how important it is, but then, they move on to their own to-do list, or get lured by the next thing that captures their attention. Meanwhile, their people are just beginning to grasp the first message, and they're still trying to figure out how they each fit into the process. Your team not only needs to hear your vision over and over again, but they need to add their ideas and concerns to it before they can get behind your proposal with any real sense of ownership.

This delay by your staff isn't because your people are dense or deaf. They're trying their best to follow, but shiny objects can also distract them. Unless you stay close to them with your ideas, and listen to their ideas they'll surely get off target, and it's because you got too far away from them. They need assurance that they're moving appropriately toward the goal and that it matters how they invest their time. They need to hear that from you—early and often.

In many organizations, I've observed a kind of "long tail" between what senior management says and what the non-executive and non-management employees eventually deliver. It takes time and concentration to ensure that what was conceived in the "head" is being executed by the "tail." An understandable dissipation of enthusiasm will result in any organizational environment, but it need not be so. I fear it's because too many leaders are vague about defining reality. And even those that do a pretty good job of defining what is relevant continually speed on to their next great idea without sticking around to water the seeds they've just planted.

I think that is why DePree went on to define the key obligations of a leader in this way: "The first responsibility of a leader is to define reality. The last is to say thank you. In between the two, the leader must become a servant and a debtor."[2]

Your responsibility is to meander through the many probable options before you drop your seeds into the soil, not afterward. Explore the broad palette of possibilities before committing to any of them, not after. Develop what Greg McGeown calls Essentialism. He says, "To discern what is truly essential we need space to think, time to look and listen, permission to play, wisdom to sleep, and the discipline to apply highly selective criteria to the choices we make."[3]

McGeown's view is very similar to the three criteria for competency outlined by the performance coaches that I discussed earlier. As a leader, you do not get to announce your decree and then waltz blissfully into your next dream (or create your employees' next nightmare.) Your obligation to your followers, and to your idea, is to remain close to your people and continually use your capability for *Differentiation* to distinguish between what is key to success and what is not. Remember, you are the one with this leadership ability because you invested all those hours becoming competent. Serve and support your team members and allow them to define the tactics required to achieve your vision.

Now roll up your sleeves so you can remove the inevitable and unforeseen obstacles and repeatedly credit your staff for their achievements. Then, once the goal is achieved, you get to relax and thank your team for their incredibly hard work, because *they* did it! Although, if you operate with a "hit and run" method of leading, you'll fail to progress in developing your *Capacity For Replication.*

Should you persist in unpacking the Inside*OUT* leadership strategy, you'll discover that you need to become adept at communicating *with*, not just *to*, those who are following you. Now is when all the inner work of *Competence* and *Differentiation* begins to break through your skin and becomes externalized. You begin to interact with others, to actually influence them. So let's look at how an Inside*OUT* leader does this.

Communication

At this stage in your developing *Influence*, you'll now want to convey your message to others. You must articulate to others what you have already so clearly defined for yourself. I'm referring here to artful speaking and artful listening since that is what connects you to your team and to your community.

Communication is a kind of communion, a common union, a shared experience. Let's take a deep dive into this pool of mutuality. If to speak means that you're *transmitting*, that you're sending, then listening is not simply *ceasing to transmit,* but rather, it means that you are actively *receiving.* This is a difficult and demanding task for most leaders, especially those who are accustomed to having individuals around them awaiting their oh-so-magnificent words.

Being quiet and attending deliberately to others requires a keen ability with language and with human understanding. But simply using the sending function of interaction isn't enough. Receiving is also required. You'll also need to astutely listen to what others are communicating, both what they say and how they say it, so that *they* feel understood.

I see two problems inherent for many leaders. First, they forget that they're usually speaking more loudly when they're silent than when they are not. Their silence forces others to make up what's being implied, and this rarely leads to an accurate or even a good outcome. Second, many leaders habitually reach for their overly used linguistic intelligence when they're around others, and consequently, they fail to stretch their interpersonal intellect in ways that could be even more influential. In other words, the opposite of speaking is not silence. It is listening.

Let's begin by examining this receiving function. First of all, it's rarely done. How do I know? Because, no doubt you're hearing a voice in your head right now that's saying something like, "What does he mean?" Or, "Not me, I'm an introvert, and I'm always listening to other people." Or, "I'm already a pretty good listener."

Regardless of the message playing in your head right now, you're still having a conversation with yourself, and you're not listening to what I'm saying. This is what we humans do most of the time. However, just because it's popular and habitual doesn't mean it's helpful. Just because you're not speaking doesn't mean that you're listening.

Now, I'm not a baseball player or even a fan of the game, but I do know a bit about the game. I know that a key part of each contest is the game that occurs between the pitcher and the catcher. These two people play on the same team and are really interested on working together to make certain that their team wins. And then there is this third player, from the other team, who stands between them and tries to disrupt this attempt at winning. And what's most incredible is that this third player carries a huge stick and often waves it at the ball. Most of the time the catcher and pitcher are able to carry on their little game without too much interference, though sometimes the other player with the stick hits the ball and disrupts their little game.

I hope baseball fans will accept my apology for having a bit of fun with "America's pastime," but I tell the story this way because it reminds me of so many conversations in which I've been one of the players. Perhaps you can identify with this. You meet up with another person to toss some ideas, proposals, or concerns back and forth, but something gets in the way of successfully ending up with a plan that you both understand and agree to. It's as if a third player steps between the two of you.

The real obstacle to understanding is that voice you each carry inside your heads. Each voice has a point-of-view and is making up pictures based on a personal viewpoint. It's almost guaranteed that you will each leave the meeting with a different set of pictures about what you discussed. By habitually settling for ineffective and inefficient conversations like these, you're hurting the important relationships with the people who matter most—your employees, your colleagues, your family, and your friends.

Listening in order to genuinely understand the other's viewpoint takes effort. It means you have to harness your intellectual capacity, especially your curiosity, to hear something you possibly don't already know, or to learn something about the other person that is outside of your entrenched assumptions. This kind of listening is not saying to the speaker, "I understand." Instead, it's conveying *what* you understand.

If, like me, you occasionally enter into a conversation already certain of where it's headed, or you think you've heard it all before, and you simply wish you could extract yourself from the conversation and move on to something you deem more important, then obviously this is not the way to learn something new, or to convey understanding, or to gain trust. Nor is it possible to continually avoid the thoughts and concerns of our loved ones or our colleagues at work. Eventually, we need to show up for the conversation.

Showing up means that you first align your intention with your body. Similar to the intent of the baseball catcher, place your body in a receiving position. If you want to play this game of conversation, you must attend to the speaker, not to your watch, or to your smart phone, or to any of the other concerns running on inside your head. Incidentally, facing the speaker directly is also a great way to keep your own mind, not just your body, open to receiving what the speaker has to deliver.

This kind of engagement means that you genuinely attempt to grasp the issue from the *speaker's* frame-of-reference. It means you briefly say back what you think the sender (the pitcher) meant to communicate. Except here is what usually occurs.

Let's imagine that you agree with the idea, and you get excited and tell the sender how much you agree and what you think about the idea. If you do anything like that, you're sending words from *your* frame-of-reference, not theirs. Or let's say you have more questions about the issue, and you engage with curiosity. While it is wonderful to have a curious partner, you are still engaging from *your* frame-of-reference. You still haven't proven to the speaker that you even grasp their idea until you can say back what you think the sender meant to communicate. You could be talking about two different things, in which case agreement or questions can be a total waste of time.

To say back what the sender is attempting to communicate means that you have to put yourself into that person's shoes. You must attempt to see through the lens they are using, whether you agree or disagree. This is really quite easy once you intend to listen.

If you just want to disagree or agree, debate or convince, learn more or demonstrate your knowledge, then you're not listening; you're reacting; you're speaking; you aren't learning, and you aren't proving your understanding. Oh, and you're also not enhancing the relationship.

This technique and skill of listening is called reflecting. It is how you clarify that what you heard is, in fact, what the sender meant to say. In my professional and personal life, this skill is hands down the most valuable instrument I have. And it is the one tool I make certain that each of my clients learns and uses. Reflecting well requires you to display mental agility, emotional flexibility, and genuine regard for the other person. When people feel heard, they are more likely to listen to you. Therefore, this skill is one of your most influential tools.

Many coaches and writers have laid out different models and tips for how to listen. And the best method that I've seen is the work of Robert Bolton in his classic book, *People Skills*.[4] Bolton not only wrote this masterful handbook for more meaningful conversations, he also formed Ridge Associates, a training and consulting organization that teaches clients how to conduct their life "on the narrow ridge that is a state of mind and heart that blends integrity, acceptance, and interpersonal skill even when dealing with contradictory opinions and values."[5]

Let me be clear. Playing the conversation game does not mean that you're always stuck behind home plate playing the position of catcher. Conversation implies give and take, sending and receiving. So for effective and productive communicating, your speaking needs to be as skillful as your listening. Here's why. If you've already achieved empathetic understanding of the other person through your listening skills, then you're much more equipped to explain yourself in a focused and tailored fashion and far less likely to say something stupid, rude, hurtful, or irrelevant.

Okay, it's time for the other side of a conversation, the speaking side. You now get to go to the pitcher's mound. The most important first step in speaking is to own your own words. Wait, you protest, isn't that what speaking is, your own words? Not necessarily.

Too often, when we're in a conversation and emotions begin to run hot, we make comments about the other person rather than saying what *we* think or especially how *we* feel about the issue. This is what I mean when I say "own your own words." Some authors have referred to this as speaking with an "I" message versus a "you" message.

Here's an example of a "you" message, "You betrayed me in the meeting." This comment will most certainly raise the other's defenses. Alternatively, an "I" message might be, "I felt betrayed in the meeting when you didn't support my proposal."

And here's another example; "You said you would finish the project by last Friday, and you dropped the ball yet again." Instead, state your own expectation, like this: "I thought that you would've completed the project by last Friday." The second message in each of these examples uses the preferred "I" message.

Consequently, if you expect to move others to buy into your *Vision*, to go along with your plans, or to even become motivated to exceed your expectations, you need to provide clear instructions or expectations when you speak. I recall a story that a colleague told many times when she was describing the importance of communicating. A senior executive had hired her to provide leadership coaching to a manager on this executive's team. She interviewed her client so that she would understand exactly what this executive wanted from his team member. Once the coach reflected what the executive told her and was certain she understood the executive's expectations, she began the coaching process with the manager. In a few weeks, she called the client to get his feedback about the manager's progress. The executive said he couldn't believe how quickly the manager had changed his behavior and was now performing flawlessly. He asked the coach what she did. She said, "I just told your manager what you told me you needed from him."

Clear *Communication* really isn't too difficult, but you can make it more complicated when you allow your own emotions to become an obstacle to attentive listening and clear speaking. We'll never know why that executive didn't simply tell the manager what he expected in the first place, but I bet he had played the conversation over in his mind so many times that he became paralyzed by the emotional possibilities and it was simply easier for him to hire a professional coach to step in. Alternatively, he might have actually had conversations with the manager but so clouded his message with his own emotional agenda that his message was unclear.

I'm not suggesting that you omit emotions from conversations but rather that you express your emotions, wisely. As a leader who wants to be influential for all the right reasons, you need to manage your own words and your own emotions, and you need to use both of them to communicate genuinely with others.

In her book, *Fierce Conversations*, renowned public speaker Susan Scott advises, "Take responsibility for your emotional wake. For a leader there is no trivial comment. Something you don't remember saying may have a devastating impact on someone who looked to you for guidance and approval. The conversation is not about the relationship; the conversation *is* the relationship. Learning to deliver the message without the load allows you to speak with clarity, conviction, and compassion."[6]

As you're developing your capacities for leading, you're probably noticing how the gains that you make in one capacity inevitably affect other areas as well. Your diligent attention to expanding your *Capacity For Self-Mastery,* which we unpacked in chapter 2, has most likely already helped you in your *Communication.* And the reverse also occurs. The growth you make in your abilities for clear and compassionate interaction adds traction and credibility to each of your other capacities.

Before you leave this stage, *Communication,* I'd like you to look at one more area that's especially critical for a leader: communicating to a large group of individuals.

Leaders often speak to their teams, or to the entire office during a lunch series, or to their Board, or to an audience at a conference. If you've practiced the art of communicating in the ways I've already discussed, then you have only a slight, though difficult, adjustment to make when you're speaking to larger groups. You must communicate *as though* your listeners are actually in conversation with you.

In his book, *The Articulate Executive,* Granville Toogood says, "Stop thinking that every time you stand up to say something you are making a speech—because you're not. What you're really doing is having an enlarged conversation— even though there may be 100 people listening, and even though you may be doing all the talking."[7] In other words, you must let your audience know that you already have a pretty good idea what they're thinking as they listen to you.

You might simply say something like this, "If I were sitting where you are, I'd be wondering how the new plan will affect my job. I'll tell you..."

Now, if you're introverted, you probably state your opinions less frequently and with less energy. Conversely, if you're someone with more social energy, you likely initiate conversations, state your point of view without being asked, and do so with a drive that can cause others to withhold their opinions, especially if you're their leader.

Your degree of awareness for how others perceive your *Communication* habits will affect how your followers understand you. In addition to your skillful listening, you can increase the odds of others actually listening to you by packaging your presentations in a way that will yield the best possible receptivity.

One of the most pointed descriptions I've ever read for how a leader should package what they have to say is from *The Articulate Executive*. Toogood says, "Leaders *add value* to what they are saying by *taking a position*. They have a *point of view*. They *translate* situations into positions. They *present evidence* to back up their position, then propose a *course of action*. *They speak simply*. They answer our objections before we can raise them. *They press the case with conviction*. They *believe*."[8]

Thus, when you speak to large groups of people, knowing your audience and taking your position accordingly will go a long way toward your ability to be influential. If you remember that communicating with a group means that there are more of them than you, then their concerns and needs come first. If you're focused only on you, on your own frame-of-reference, others are likely to pick that up and tune out or turn against you.

However, most of the time you're meeting with smaller groups or you're communicating one-on-one. Each of Toogood's descriptions for being articulate are important and will require you to be focused on how you're communicating regardless of audience size. As you become more skillful and natural with your *Communication,* you will also be more at ease and the real you will simply be present.

If you already have an authentic charismatic style, just continue to be you and add these behaviors to your repertoire. And if you're not naturally a captivating speaker, don't worry; you really don't need to drastically change either. Just continue being who you are and simply add a few behaviors that will expand your capacity.

In a study examining the effects of leader humility on employee morale and turnover, which is certainly something that you'll want to consider when expanding your *Capacity for Replication*, Bradley Owens and colleagues found that, "…In contrast to rousing employees through charismatic, energetic, and idealistic leadership approaches (…) a 'quieter' leadership approach, with listening, being transparent about limitations, and appreciating follower strengths and contributions [is the most] effective way to engage employees."9

Now that you've expanded your many techniques of *Communication*, it's time to uncork your *Influence* and intentionally pour yourself into the lives of others. This kind of dedication means that you'll create future leaders, not merely more followers.

Reproduction

At this stage in your *Capacity For Replication*, you'll begin to feel the desire to turn your attention toward leaving a legacy. Perhaps you're triggered by your own loyal watchfulness over the organization's long-term viability, or maybe you're enthusiastic about a group of budding leaders, or possibly you have a creeping sense of professional mortality. Whatever the prompts, you become aware that you indeed want to have something to leave for those who will be coming after you. No, this isn't a tax-protected trust of some sort, though you might choose to include that in your generosity as well. Rather, this is a pouring out of your knowledge and your lessons-learned back into the great ocean from which your own experience came.

To really care about your organization, you must look beyond the next quarter's targets or even the next year's goals. You must look ahead as far as you can possibly see, into and beyond the five and ten year plans. This sort of care requires that you specifically identify and promote both the active and the hidden leadership skills in others. As an influential leader, you must become attuned to your positional impermanence, and you must vigorously bring high potential people into the tasks and positions that will make them the next effective leaders. This capability should be quite easy because you've already familiarized yourself with the essential elements of professional expertise through your

Competence, your ability to focus on what is important for a protégé to develop through *Differentiation,* and you've improved your *Communication.*

As an experienced leader, you might also want to make the path a bit clearer for the up-and-coming supervisor. You might do this by revealing the details of the industry or even the quirks of your organization. You're providing a map of the pitfalls, bruises, delays, and politics that you experienced. Remember though, you're only offering a map, not the actual journey. We each learn best through experience, our own.

A few of my client organizations have created formal programs or promoted casual connections in which first-time managers and seasoned supervisors are paired. In this way, new managers can more quickly and surely navigate the inevitable challenges they are likely to face.

Though, in some industries, this kind of relationship has gained more prominence in recent years, it is by no means innovative. For centuries, the crafts and the arts have prospered from the labors of an apprentice who worked with a master. This practice has evolved into career paths utilized by labor unions, artist guilds, and even in the progression from college student to graduate student. Germans use this mentoring process in many industries, and companies like BMW and Mercedes-Benz have also imported their well-thought-through staff development procedures to their facilities here in the U.S.

As an Inside*OUT* leader, you already know that reproducing your *skills* is only a part of the process. You want to produce people who are also well-rounded individuals and who might become even more effective leaders than you have been. At this stage of *Reproduction,* you don't merely maintain safekeeping of your own position, but you seek an even greater level of mastery for the next generation.

This special component is what's been cooked into the best and most influential leaders for millennia. Remember Homer's *Odyssey*? The classical retelling of this ancient epic poem mainly focuses on the Greek hero Ulysses, king of Ithaca, and his journey home after the fall of Troy. Before he even left for the campaign, he had entrusted his young son, Telemachus, to a protective, guiding, and supportive figure who acted as a wise and trusted counselor.[10] While scholars might still debate this person's actual effectiveness in his role with the young boy, what remains in our modern vocabulary is his name, Mentor.

As an Inside*OUT* leader, you'll begin to experience some characteristics of each of your capacities flowing from you and into others. Except you shouldn't wait for Ulysses or other royalty to intervene and assign you to become a tutor. You'll want your *Influence* to overflow early and often so that your bequest will live on in the lives of individuals in your organization and in your community.

Reproduction is one of the ways that you can notice how your other leadership capacities combine with your skills to make it possible for your followers to eventually stand on your shoulders. There, they can see further, gain deeper insight, and achieve greater triumphs. You see, *Reproduction* is not just a task force you assemble, a program that you sponsor, or a one-time volunteer assignment that you fulfill. No, for your *Influence* to be fully experienced by others, you need to serve those who will succeed you.

I have frequently asked managers and supervisors in my training courses if they consider themselves a leader. And because of the timing of my question and the grin on my face, they usually play along and respond with some hesitant reply like, "Well, yes, isn't this a leadership program?" Or, "Of course, I'm manager of XYZ."

Then I say, "Take your title or position out of the equation. Now, how do you know that you're a leader?"

For me the answer is very simple. If no one is willingly following, you are not a leader. Similarly, as a leader, if you are not serving the individuals in your organization, you are not a leader. You're just a boss.

Early in my training and consulting career, I was part of a team that was privileged to work with top managers in a large corporation after the CEO decided he needed to shake up the leadership structure. He thought that too many of his senior executives had become too concerned with their own security, and because of this, they were no longer placing the customer first. He noticed how this attitude was becoming pervasive in the organization. Entirely too many vise presidents and senior directors were acting like little emperors.

This CEO decided to take his senior team on a retreat to outline his plan. He explained his vision by showing their pyramid-shaped organizational chart, the one with himself at the top, and then he inverted it. He told his lieutenants that his new job description was only one line..."I am here to serve each of you." Furthermore, he invited each of these other highly paid individuals to look at their own organizations and to do likewise.

Perhaps the most startling disclosure was when he added that if anyone was unwilling to follow his lead and could not take a similar stance in their organizations, he would do everything he could to help them flourish elsewhere. This was not a threat; he simply differentiated between how it was and how it was going to be. He was serious about serving, and he was willing to actually assist those who could not join him in this organization-wide refocus. He leveraged his *Influence* to make certain that each of the leaders who did not accept his challenge landed a worthy position with a different employer. He would insure that they too could still thrive.

Putting yourself on the line like this CEO takes high-capacity guts—it requires both clarity and a willingness to be transparent. When you're prepared to play your hand with all your chips on the table, then you experience an intense energy that is reserved for those individuals who others eagerly follow.

Incidentally, nearly every one of that CEO's lieutenants followed his lead. The company's revenues went from flat growth prior to the CEO's shakeup, to a hockey stick curve after the organization-wide refocus. He led by serving, others followed, and the corporation prospered.

How would you continue to play after you've laid down such a massive gamble? How do you keep yourself and the organization vibrant when you approach your work with an "all-in" attitude? First of all, you cannot do it alone and that is why you must replicate yourself. Before you place your wager, you need to insure that your organization has a dynamic succession plan and that you have a well defined personal plan as well; a plan that requires you to infuse your skills, knowledge, and values into the lives of those who will become the next leaders. And that brings us to our next stage in *Influence*.

Stewardship

Your *Capacity for Replication* will become fully developed when you attend equally to refining both your own abilities as well as those of your followers. The leader who no longer stretches but rests on already achieved accomplishments devalues his *Influence*. Therefore, as you continue to grow into *Stewardship*, you must become vigilant in caring for and feeding the emerging abilities of those who will take your place in this or in some other organization. You're not merely preparing a protégé to serve your own organization. You're fostering a better and more skillfully led community as well.

When I proposed to executives and supervisors that they invest in and train their people to be the best technicians, customer service reps, teachers, or managers, they often chafed at my suggestion, and they pushed back with, "Yeah, I invest in them, and then they walk for a better deal." These executives feared they would then lose their own highly trained personnel to their competition.

And I say, "That's right, so? You've always gone for the better deal yourself, so you can't fault others." And when we increase the skill level of people in our employ, we're raising the bar for skills, for wages, and for quality within our industry and in our community. Regardless, if they stay or leave, you ultimately win.

Wouldn't you rather work, live, shop, worship, and recreate in a community where individuals are treasured in their workplaces and valued by their leaders than the alternative? Just imagine the possible consequences if your mechanic, while repairing your car, is distracted by the grumbling and shouting on the shop floor? Or worse yet, if the nurse who is responsible for your care is preoccupied with a labor shortage, salary dispute, or policy change where benefits are reduced? Wouldn't you willingly pay the higher prices for services delivered and for goods produced by individuals who receive a living wage and who work in a organization that truly values them?

As a leader, you have an obligation to the betterment of your employees. Employees should have some way to grow and develop within an industry or profession, either through continuing education for job advancement or more formal education for career development and life expansion. As a steward, you will guarantee that your followers have the benefit of ongoing education and development.

We no longer exist within a feudal system of masters and lords or of apprentices and journeymen. Your most aspiring workers will change careers and even try different industries or disciplines many times during their working lives. Leaders must continually empty themselves into the next generation, so we can all benefit from the collective and ever-evolving advances in our industries and professions. *Stewardship* means you understand that your position of leadership is a temporary role, one that is survived by the permanency of your organization. Embracing *Stewardship* means that you're insuring your organization's future strength.

One inspiring example of *Stewardship* comes from the story behind the Chicago Cubs winning of the 2016 World Series of baseball. The president of the club, Theo Epstein, who had already experienced the transitory taste of success in guiding the Boston Red Sox to two World Series wins, realized that if he were to go beyond his achievements he would need to expand in his own leadership capacities.

In his book, *The Cubs Way,* Tom Verducci explains how Epstein's own development as a leader prepared him to produce a team in Chicago that won the World Series championship after more than a 100-year dry spell. Back in Boston, Epstein had introduced cutting edge, data-driven analytics to the process of recruiting and developing his players. He maintained the use of those techniques. Meanwhile, he learned a deeper and more ancient truth that he brought with him in his move to Chicago. Epstein said.

> Interestingly, during the push for the next competitive advantage and how flat everything's gotten now and how smart everyone is, and how everyone is using basically the same technology, I feel like I've pushed our organization [Chicago Cubs] back to the human being. And thankfully so.

> If we can't find the next technological breakthrough, well, maybe we can be better than anyone else with how we treat our players and how we connect with players and the relationships we develop and how we put them in positions to succeed. Maybe our environment will be the best in the game, maybe our vibe will be the best in the game, maybe our players will be the loosest, and maybe they'll have the most fun and maybe they'll care the most. It's impossible to quantify.[11]

Epstein is an example of a leader who realized that the latest processes, systems, and software would soon merge into the next update. He also knew that it's the collective character of the people that's embodied in an organization's zeitgeist that lives on. It is the organization's people who endure.

Epstein was maturing as a leader and realized that his own capacity for leading was critical to the team's success. Many leaders would take credit for wins or assign blame for failures anywhere but on themselves. The Inside*OUT* leader takes replication seriously and conscientiously curates the resources available.

You've already established your own abilities. As a steward, you must also care for the abilities of others. First, your attention must be on individual well-being; you must do everything within your authority to make certain that your people are safe in their working environments. You need to be focusing on each of your employees and taking action toward making their work experience one of happiness, satisfaction, and fulfillment.

While concentrating on individuals is necessary, it's not sufficient at this level of leadership. You must also deal with clusters of individuals. Each team or work group is a unique subculture. You're responsible for creating and maintaining the kinds of cultures within your organization that support your values and your intentions. Epstein called it chemistry; you might call it the culture or simply the way team members relate to each other. Regardless, it's what shapes the final product or service that emerges from your organization. In order for your teams to succeed, it's important that any internal upset, lack of motivation, or team conflict doesn't infect the team's interaction with other teams or with your customers and clients.

We now live and work in a global culture, one in which our organizations, and even our nations, are merely subcultures. With these expanded capacities, you must learn to deal with the complexities of so many differences. In fact, if you restrict or resist the unfamiliar, you do so at the cost of the probable growth and contribution of the organization to worldwide needs.

During the 2015 McDonald Cadet Leadership Conference at West Point, one of the study groups focused on *Stewardship* concluded.

> The more involved organizations become with different cultures, the more responsible they become for all kinds of people. The key to success is to become a *globally conscious steward*—a steward of the vision you were entrusted with; of the livelihoods of those in your organization; and now, of the welfare of the global community. This suggests a need for a culturally competent set of organizational values that is adjusted to the globalizing world.[12]

Of course, this is easier and more likely when teams and individuals are already working well within the organization.

Coda

It had been several years since I heard from Lars. Then one morning, I discovered a wonderful email from him about his new position, his latest pride and joy. He had returned from another overseas assignment about a year earlier and took charge of a new division for the company as Vice President of Global Quality and Effectiveness. I secretly wondered if this would become another opportunity for me to work alongside one of my protégés.

We arranged a Skype chat in which he quickly said that he wasn't looking to schedule me for more of my input. Instead, he wanted to tell me how he had brought his global team together over the past months to work as a cohesive unit for the benefit of the clients they served. He was just staying in contact with me.

I think it was at that moment that the notion of my own

Influence hit me. Here was Lars, not sounding like a client but like the corporate leader he had become. He described the processes he had already undertaken to develop his team and what he was doing to help his team deal with the current turmoil in their industry. During the call, he thanked me several times for mentoring him when he had no one else to turn to and when it appeared to everyone as if he didn't need any help. I couldn't help but smile inside as I imagined the very real prospect that Lars would someday soon receive a similar call from one of the many emerging leaders he has mentored.

Your last act of *Stewardship* is to remain on the stage for as long as you still have your song inside. So throw back your head, take a deep breath, sing it out, and empty yourself of all those lessons, skills, and wisdom that you developed in your career. You have a legacy. Give it away. Someone needs it.

We shall not cease from exploration,

and the end of all our exploring

will be to arrive where we started

and know the place for the first time.

—T.S. Eliot

9

*OUT*COMES

Turned Inside*OUT*

Whew, you made it. You took a huge step by committing to learn how to expand your capabilities to lead, especially if you're someone who doesn't usually pick up a book like this. On the other hand, this might be your sixth business/leadership book that you've already read this year, and you're proud of your self-designed course of study. Or you might just be at the threshold of your leadership career, and you found your way to this material and have not yet read other books about leading. Regardless of how you've arrived, I'm glad you're here.

Let's briefly look back at how you got here, how you expanded your capacities to lead. You began by expanding your Capacity for Self-Mastery. You discovered what it means to be the maestro of your own inner orchestra, to compose your life with purpose, and to have a cause. Then you learned how to be comfortable in your own skin so you could create relationships with others at a deep level, and you learned to move through your world with confidence because you developed impeccable social currency and had nothing to hide.

You continued your journey by exhibiting forward-looking enthusiasm that infused others with the desire to achieve the impossible. You didn't only stretch your emotional bandwidth, you also explored unfamiliar ways of knowing with a curiosity that expanded the bounds of what you thought you already knew. And you did all this with an energy that made it possible for you to be fully present to your own and to others' predicaments. It was through this incredible journey of recreating yourself that you then became able to pour yourself into those who will follow in your wake. You became a steward of your organization's future.

Within each capacity, each stage of your development encompassed and transcended the attributes and capabilities of the previous stages. And as you attended to your personal and professional development within a specific capacity, every other capacity expanded as well.

You may now take your place amongst the other individuals who lead with greater and more resilient leadership capacities. You've joined the cadre of leaders who have turned themselves Inside*OUT*. These leaders are now known in their organizations and in their communities as individuals who radiate the highest attributes of each capacity: *Self-Mastery, Affinity, Civility, Vitality, Wisdom, Presence, and Stewardship.*

By progressing through the capacities, you discovered that the first two stages of each capacity are experienced internally. They were totally invisible except to you. Then in the third stage, your growth became visible to others as you began to express your evolving self. In stages four and five, your progress became even more external and rippled outward into ever-larger waves of impact. The effect of your growth ultimately influenced your organization and eventually spread into the communities that you and your organization serve.

What a journey!

Setting a High Standard

If there's one trait that typifies a leader with these expanded capacities, it's generosity. Their spirit has become large enough to realize that everything isn't all about them. Their efforts are best realized in service to others.

This trait doesn't only describe mature individuals, but businesses and organizations can also be incubators for generosity depending on the capacities of its leadership. In the heyday of the American industrial era, some industrial leaders became prominent benefactors. Philanthropy emerged, and then schools, hospitals, and libraries sprouted in many cities and towns. Today we have tech innovators and market investors who are leading us into the future with their generosity. Elon Musk, Warren Buffett, Bill and Melinda Gates, and George Soros are just a few of the names we recognize because they have turned their attention toward taking on some of the larger challenges in our society.

While these acts of philanthropy don't prove evolved leadership, the reverse is true—seasoned Inside*OUT* leaders generously pour their resources into others and into causes that matter to them and to society. Their primary attribute is selflessness, an absence of ego. They're focused on using whatever influence they can to lift everyone up.

Think about former President Jimmy Carter, who will be ninety-four years old in 2018, truly an elder statesman. From founding the Carter Center as a vehicle for his commitment to human rights to wearing a hard hat and using a hammer to build houses with Habitat for Humanity, he continues to serve others in whatever capacity he can. He clearly is not interested in amassing wealth and prestige for his own benefit but to use his influence for the advancement of others.

Another person who was not originally considered a leader but has become one nonetheless, Oprah Winfrey, exhibits the traits of a person dedicated to a set of core values. From her wise decisions in building her brand and business empire to serving her followers and the less fortunate throughout the world, she is a paragon of philanthropy and mentorship. She's also an example of servant leading in the practical ways she supports and assists her employees. And many regard her as a transformational leader because of how she inspires and elevates others. Here's an example of someone who just kept choosing her choices.

Now It's Your Turn

If you've not only read this book, but you've also deeply engaged with the progression of your own leadership development throughout this material by planning and observing your own growth steps and by choosing your expansion based on the twists and turns of your organization, then here is what's next for you. Now you are leading from behind and empowering those in the front to become Inside*OUT* leaders, and you're about to step into another dimension of leadership.

As an Inside*OUT* leader, you now have the responsibility to use your own experiences and the road maps that you employed and discovered while studying this material to lift your organization to its wholeness. What you've already achieved with yourself at the individual level can now be applied at the organizational level. You've already conducted your own growth in this Inside*OUT* process, and you're now equipped to take on the challenges of guiding an organization to its full potential. This next project will be similar to the journey shown on the map of your individual process but vastly different in scale and complexity.

The fifth stage in each of your expanded capacities connects to what Jim Collins describes in his book *Good to Great*. He suggests that the highest level of executive capabilities reveals the dual traits of humility + will, qualities we often deem contradictory or even impossible, especially among business and political leaders. How mature leaders express these attributes makes this combination unique. He writes, "[These] leaders channel their ego needs away from themselves and into the larger goal of building a great company. It's not that [these] leaders have no ego or self-interest. Indeed, they are incredibly ambitious—*but their ambition is first and foremost for the institution, not themselves.*"[1]

You're now full; you're at capacity. Even though you've already transferred some discoveries from your own growth to energize and influence the growth of others, as an Inside*OUT* leader you're now expected to completely pour yourself into the next generation. You'll no longer care about the tributes and the acclaim that your fans toss in your direction. No, now you're more interested in making sure that the company or the organization gets the credit for successes. Your interests are fully focused on taking nothing with you but instead to leave your team in a better place.

As you reflect back on your own journey, you might even be curious if it would be possible for an organization to follow a similar road map for expanding its capacity for significance. You care about your organization, and you want it to become a frontrunner in its methods, in its market, and in its mission.

Considerations Before You Begin

Before you suit up for the job, there are four key factors to consider as you expand your focus from the personal to the scale of the organizational.

First, just as you encountered a large number of interacting subpersonalities within your own journey, you'll discover that your organization is also made up of layers of interacting systems. Some will be quite obvious, and many will be obscure. You'll benefit from identifying these early on. Look at the processes and the dynamics among the various functions instead of focusing on the individuals or departments. In other words, look at the forest's sunlight, water, and critters, the ecosystem, not just the trees.

Second, remember how difficult it was to decipher the vague, partial, or even incomprehensible information arising from your own inner dynamics? Similarly, interactions among the systems within your organization are intricately linked. Yet they're linked in ways that can cause small changes to produce disproportionately large effects. So stay awake, be vigilant and responsive to new data. For example, if you change the expense reporting process to a smoother accounting process for the finance department, you also need to consider the impact on the sales force and the field offices.

And third, just as you've discovered how often your best solutions have ultimately come from within yourself, so it is in your organization. Its most valuable solutions will emerge from the dynamics within the system and cannot be reliably imposed from outside. In order to generate its own unique outcomes, you actually become the organization's maestro, not its boss, or even its creator. Study the issue before you engage an outside consultant, not afterward.

And here's the final guideline. Keep looking forward. As you evolved, you didn't look to the past for your path-to-the-future. Instead, you linked your *Imagination* to a durable *Vision* of what you could become. In a similar way, your organization will need to become openly curious about what is possible rather than maintain a grip on its past. This doesn't imply that you forget the past, just that you don't grasp onto it as if it's a certain predictor of your future. The dynamic nature of technology, of markets, of global scale, and of economic inequality means that you need agile leaders who will keep your collective sights on the horizon of possibility versus the memories of a certain past.

Creating An Inside*OUT* Organization

I admit these are big questions to ask about your company or your organization, and there's a part of my brain that begins to go numb at the magnitude of possibilities. However, to persist in this work, you must collaborate with others who are also drawn toward these notions.

Let's apply the Inside*OUT* model and speculate what might happen in your organization if it were to develop along the same lines as you have. To begin, consider the possible answers to the three cosmic questions that you asked yourself as you expanded your *Identity*, your *Capacity for Self-Mastery;* who am I, why am I here, and where am I going? What kind of descriptions would you use or would you need to create to even come close to describing an organization that's comprised of more unifying dynamics than the fragmenting terms we now use, words like divisions, departments, or even teams? What kind of unifying and cohering force fields would be required in order for the organization to function as an organism with coordinated and responsive systems? Instead of performing under the direction of a person, its maestro, what cohering and impersonal force would guide this organization?

Can you imagine what an organization like this might declare as its reason for existence, its purpose? And can you imagine the energy that would be unleashed through this organization because it's so focused on its cause, its mission?

These are colossal considerations, not ones to answer in one sitting, or perhaps even one lifetime. Though, if you can hold onto possibilities like these, you just might be prepared to recognize the answers when they appear. I've heard this called "living in the question."

Exploring the answers to these questions merely investigates the organization's *Identity*; then, you'll have the following six additional capacities to consider as well. Let's do that right now. Let's look at each capacity and then look to some organizations that are wrestling with these questions.

Insight—Capacity for Connection. How might you create a failsafe feedback loop so that your organization can know itself intimately; so that it resists getting caught in perpetual self-improvement and re-branding because its purpose is too small for the next generation of human evolution; and so that it always uses its energies to enhance the human connections amongst its employees, its customers and clients, and its sustainable relationships with the ecosystems? Patagonia is one example of a company that works diligently to use its values to guide its product development, supply chain management, and even to guide the way it treats its staff, its customers, and the planet.

Integrity—Capacity for Transparency. What would it take for your organization to function in a way that would make regulations, oversight, and policing a thing of the past? Could your organization exceed the standards in your industry, the laws of various Federal regulatory agencies, human standards enshrined in the Universal Declaration of Human Rights, and perhaps even initiate a Declaration for Planetary Rights? One example in this direction is Johnson & Johnson's citizenship and sustainability approach that's inextricably linked to their vision of a world and their Credo where a healthy mind, body, and environment are within reach for everyone, everywhere.

Inspiration—Capacity for Innovation. You're probably already working on ways for your organization to increase or expand its products and services. Can you imagine how your organization itself could evolve or morph into a new entity? No, I'm not referring to opening your third restaurant, or acquiring a competitor, or even adding new product lines, though each of these are ways you might grow. Rather, how could your organization transform itself? Perhaps an organization owned entirely by employees, a group of people aligned behind a common mission with a commitment that embodies its values through every cell of its being? One simple example is New Belgium Brewing Company, an employee owned and managed company in Fort Collins, Colorado, that also happens to produce great beer.

Intelligence—Capacity for Perception. Where is the brain, the central nervous system of your organization? Does it reside in the C-level offices, the staff cubicles, or on the shop floor? Or is it in all these places and more? Most importantly, do you know where its brains are? How could your organization be curious and nimble while simultaneously forging smart systems? How might it promote new ideas and create a free flow of information? How could it not only meet customers' current needs but also create a market where one never existed before? What would it take to disrupt its "business as usual" and imagine new ways to be in relationship with its customers? Many in Silicon Valley consider this kind of innovation to be the path to creating new markets. Netflix, Airbnb, Tesla Motors, Amazon, Google, and

Apple are just a few companies that are disrupting their industries.

Initiative—Capacity for Action. What might happen in your organization if individuals weren't compelled to look busy or to produce the work of three other individuals as well as their own work? What if they based their activities on purposeful choices? What would need to change in the supervisory processes in order for personnel to have actual autonomy in their work? Or what would it require for your organization to be a force in your industry that is not based on square footage, head count, or profit margins but rather on simply being an enduring presence? One example is the persistent efforts of the organic food industry to pressure Big Food and the U.S. Department of Agriculture. One company in particular, Amy's Kitchen, has been at the table since its beginning in 1987 with a steadfast commitment to choose what's best for their customers, their farmers, their employees, and the planet.

Influence—Capacity for Replication. What would it look like if, instead of vanquishing or purchasing its competitors, your organization knew that it was really good at what it does and so it created other autonomous organizations to help the competitors become even better? What if your company operated like a seed bank instead of an insatiable hoarder? What if along with delivery of the product or service from your team, you began to market your methods, your philosophy, or your secrets? How open would the organization's heart need to be in order to shift its business model from competition to cooperation? One example is IDEO, the international design and consulting firm headquartered in Palo Alto, California. Its multidisciplinary, human-centered approach to solving complex challenges has institutionalized the many ways that humans learn and process knowledge. And they are teaching their clients and other consultants how to do the same thing.

Bon Voyage

Imagine you're the captain of a space ship in the twenty-first century. Your ship carries its cargo deep in the hearts and minds of its crew. In fact, in your mind, the ship is the crew. The ship is nothing without the totality of the people, the organization. Then you hear about an innovation that would make living, working, and being a part of this enterprise more fulfilling for everyone. You hear about a specially crafted element that can be incorporated into the very fiber of this group. It's called the Inside*OUT* leader. And you chose to become that person.

The function of your leadership is similar to that of the glass prism. Leaders must have the appropriate internal characteristics in order to fulfill their duty. They must inhabit the place in an organization where they can be most effective. And leaders must constantly hone and maintain their skills to guide their organizations and the people they lead.

Just as a deck prism is designed to multiply the quantity of light that passes through it, you are now that transparent and generous maestro through which the organization's potential can be realized.

You've focused on the qualities that make a leader, the development of your potential, and your *capacities* to lead.

May you have fair winds for your voyage.

ACKNOWLEDGMENTS

This book would not have been possible if so many persons had not generously given of themselves. Some of these individuals were simply doing their jobs and were entirely unaware of the effect they were having on me. Others were following their dreams and passions and impressed me through their commitment to their vision. Some were on their own quest and included me on their journey. Still others didn't even know me but diligently articulated their ideas in ways that profoundly influenced me. And some of these persons even paused in their own life flow to foster possibilities in me even when I couldn't see the same.

I'm grateful for their influence on me and for the opportunities and challenges each of them gave to me so that I could become clear about my contribution in this exciting world of our shared experiences of leading and following.

Thanks to my parents who always modeled leading with compassion. And to my brother, John, who forged innovative ways to preserve others' independence—especially in the smallest details of more livable communities for those "over fifty-five."

Thanks to my children who experienced my earliest efforts at leadership. I'm proud that each of them have found something from those days to duplicate, and I'm equally thrilled that they have been wise enough to distinguish, and loving enough to forgive, my errors in leading as their dad. They continually inspire me with their entrepreneurial creativity, their relational commitment, and their willingness to remake themselves.

Thanks to my teachers; Vivian King who introduced me to the practical and transformative discipline of the self: Tom Yeomans who included me in his explorations of how a group functions so that I could experience his leading in cooperation with the group's highest purpose: Roberto Assagioli who conceived of and articulated the higher functioning and potential of the psyche during a time when his peers where codifying psychological pathologies: Ken Wilber who has given so many maps and models for understanding the heights and depths of the individual spirit through his brilliant and prolific mind.

Thanks to Betsy Westendorf for the many hours of working side-by-side to bring creative and deeply meaningful solutions to

Prism's clients. And saying thank you doesn't even come close to the depth of my gratitude for the hours spent correcting my grammar and erratic punctuation, and helping me bring sense and flow to my thoughts.

Thanks to my colleagues; Robert and Dorothy Bolton for their innovative leadership in the arena of understanding through listening: Rick Brandon for his bold and witty writings about how the savvy can survive: Alex Grimshaw for trusting me enough to participate in the Executive Leadership Institute and for experimenting with these ideas while leading a global organization of committed consultants: Kelly Fairbairn who worked tirelessly to promote my skills with clients: and thanks to each of my professional colleagues who co-facilitated with me for helping me learn even more than we taught.

Thanks to each of my clients, for bringing their professional challenges to me and for trusting my guidance. Each of them came to me focused on growing themselves and in bettering their situations but they couldn't have realized how much they gave to me through their openness, confidences, and willingness to try new ways of leading.

Thanks to Deb Dunn for her voice of experience and for guiding me through the hazards and the opportunities of self-publishing.

Thanks to Marie Chancellor and to my nephew John W. Kolb for their designers' eyes that made the book's cover vivid and memorable.

Thanks to my dear friend, Peter Friedrichs, who gave me a most precious gift by believing that I had something inside that needed to be expressed and walked with me until it became real in my words and in my vocation. And then he had the courage to join me in the Executive Leadership Institute experiment.

Merci beaucoup mon amour, to my partner, Serena, for her tolerance of my escape to my office to write, and her acceptance of that far-off look in my eyes when she knew I was actually thinking through the material for this book, and for her unwavering support for me and for us. I've always felt her steadfast and deep love for me from the moment she declared, "He's with me."

RESOURCES

The following rights holders have generously given permission to use excerpts from copyrighted works listed in the following pages:

Axialent Inc.

Barrett-Koehler, Inc.

BenBella Books

Bob Rosen, author

Center for Creative Leadership

Chris Kalman, author

Daniel Coyle, author

Gretchen Sliker, author.

Hachette Book Group

HarperCollins Publishers

Harvard Business Publishing

Howard Gardner, author

Instituto Psicosintesi

John Wiley and Sons, and Jossey-Bass

McGraw-Hill Education

Michael O'Brien, author

Penguin Random House

SelectBooks, Inc.

Simon & Schuster, Inc.

TED

The Guardian

Zondervan

NOTES

Chapter 1: InsideOUT Leaders
1. Joe Flower, "A Conversation with Ronald Heifetz: Leadership without Easy Answers," The Healthcare Forum Journal 38, no. 4 (1995): 30-36, http://www6.miami.edu/pld/article_on_adaptive _change.pdf
2. Ram Charan, Stephen J. Drotter, and James Noel, *The Leadership Pipeline: How to Build the Leadership Powered Company.* 2nd ed. (San Francisco: Jossey-Bass, 2011), 37

Chapter 2: Identity
1. Gretchen Sliker, *Multiple Mind: Healing the Split in Psyche and World,* (Boston, Mass.: Shambhala, 1992), 1-2
2. Fernando Pessoa, *The Book of Disquiet.* https://www .goodreads.com/author/quotes/7816.FernandoPessoa
3. Richard Warren, *The Purpose Driven Life,* (Grand Rapids, Michigan: Zondervan, 2012), 36
4. Wes Moore, *The Work: My Search for a Life That Matters,* (New York: Random House, 2014), xxi
5. Ibid. xiv
6. Richard J. Leider and David A. Shapiro, *Work Reimagined,* (Oakland, California: Berrett-Koehler Publishers, 2015), 5
7. Ibid. 5
8. Fred Kofman and Peter Senge, "Communities of Commitment: The Heart of Learning Organizations," Axialent Inc. 2010.p.9. http://www.axialent.com/uploads/paper/archivo/Communities_of Commitment_by_Fred_Kofman.pdf

Chapter 3: Insight
1. Chris Kalman, "The Journey Within," podcast audio, Dirtbag Diaries, http://www.dirtbagdiaries.com/shorts-journey-within/
2. Carol Dweck, *Mindset: the New Psychology of Success* (New York: Ballantine Books, 2006), 4
3. Ibid. 7
4. Warren Bennis, *On Becoming A Leader* (Philadelphia, PA: Perseus Books Group, 2009), 35
5. Ibid. 36
6. "Driving Performance: How Leadership Development Powers Sustained Success." Center for Creative Leadership. May 2016. https://www.ccl.org/articles/white-papers/driving-performance-how-leadership-development-powers-sustained-success/
7. Jean-Jacques Rousseau, "The Social Contract." https:// www.goodreads .com/work/quotes/702720-du-contrat-social-ou-principes-du-droit-politique

8. Mahatma Gandhi, *The Essential Gandhi: An Anthology of His Writings on His Life, Work, and Ideas,* ed.Louis Fischer (New York: Random House, Inc., 1983), 278
9. Parker J. Palmer, *Let Your Life Speak: Listening for the Voice of Vocation* (San Fancisco, California: Jossey-Bass, 2000), 104
10. Tim Jarvis in discussion with the author, May 2017.
11. Tim Jarvis, *Chasing Shackleton* (New York: HarperCollins Publishers, 2013), 3
12. Ibid. 9
13. Ibid. 192
14. Nicholas Watt, "George Mitchell's Patient Diplomacy Shepherded Northern Ireland to Peace. Now for the Middle East..." *The Guardian,* January 23, 2009, https://www.theguardian.com/politics/blog/2009/jan/23 /george-mitchell-interview
15. Joan Halifax, "Compassion and the True Meaning of Empathy," TEDWomen video, filmed December 2010, https://www. ted.com /talks/joan_halifax
16. Bob Rosen, *Grounded: How Leaders Stay Rooted in an Uncertain World,* (Executive Summary, RHR Enterprises, 2015). http://healthycompanies.com/wpcontent/uploads /2013/08/GROUNDED-Executive-Summary-new.pdf2
17. Robert Waldinger, "What Makes A Good Life? Lessons from the Longest Study on Happiness," video, *TEDxBeaconStreet,* filmed November 2015, https://www.ted.com/talks/robert_waldinger_ what_makes_a_good_life_lessons_from_the_longest_study_on_ happiness
18. Parker J. Palmer, *Healing the Heart of Democracy: The Courage to Create a Politics Worthy of the Human Spirit* (San Francisco, California: Jossey-Bass, 2011), 31

Chapter 4: Integrity
1. Palmer, *Let Your Life Speak:,* 78
2. Nina Burrowes, "Think Authenticity Is About Being Honest and Open? Think Again." *The Guardian,* April 11, 2014, https://www.theguardian.com/women-in-leadership/2014/apr/11/ real-meaning-authenticity-leadership
3. Clare Graves, "Human Nature Prepares for a Momentous Leap." http://spiraldynamicsintegral.nl/wp-content/uploads/2013/09/ Graves-Clare-Human-Nature-Prepares-for-a-Momentous-Leap.pdf
4. Ibid.
5. Ibid.

6. Tomas Chamorro-Premuzic, "The Dark Side of Executive Narcissism: How CEOs Destroy Companies' Reputation and Employee Morale," *The Huffington Post,* January 2, 2014, http://www.huffingtonpost.com/tomas-chamorropremuzic-phd/the-dark-side-of-executiv_b_4462127.html

7. Ritchie King, Roberto Ferdman, "How many months it takes an average worker to earn what the CEO makes in an hour," *Quartz,* https://qz.com/156522/how-many-months-it-takes-an-average-worker-to-earn-what-the-ceo-makes-in-an-hour/

8. Sorapop Kiatpongsan and Michael I. Norton. "How Much (More) Should CEOs Make? A Universal Desire for More Equal Pay." *Perspectives on Psychological Science* 9, no. 6 (November 2014): 587–593

9. Brett Litz, Nathan Stein, Eileen Delaney, Leslie Lebowitz, William P. Nash, Caroline Silva, Shira Maguen, "Moral Injury and Moral Repair In War Veterans: A Preliminary Model," *Clinical Psychology Review 29,* issue 8, December 2009: 695–706, doi:10.1016/j.cpr.2009.07.003. PMID 19683376.

10. David Wood, "A Warrior's Moral Dilemma," *Huffington Post,* March 18-20, 2014, http://projects.huffingtonpost.com/projects/moral-injury

11. Chamorro-Premuzic, "The Dark Side of Executive Narcissism"

12. The Institute for Civility in Government, "What Is Civility," accessed July 2017, http://www.instituteforcivility.org/who-we-are/what-is-civility/

13. Christine Porath, Christine Pearson, "The Price of Incivility," *Harvard Business Review,* January-February 2013, https://hbr.org/2013/01/the-price-of-incivility

Chapter 5: Inspiration

1. Lance Secretan, *Inspire; What Great Leaders Do* (Hoboken, New Jersey, John Wiley & Sons, Inc., 2004) xxviii, xxix

2. David Foster Wallace, "David Foster Wallace on John McCain," *Rolling Stone, April 13, 2000.* https://www.rollingstone.com/politics/features/david-foster-wallace-on-john-mccain-2000-rolling- stone-story-w493273

3. Daniel Coyle, "How to Light a Fire: The Keith Richards Method," Daniel Coyle (blog), November 17, 2010. http://danielcoyle.com/2010/11/17/how-to-light-a-fire-the-keith-richards-method/

4. David Whyte, *The Heart Aroused* (New York: Doubleday, 1994), 80

5. Walter Isaacson, *The Innovators* (New York: Simon & Schuster, 2014), 5

6. Albert Einstein, *Cosmic Religion: With Other Opinions and Aphorisms* (Mineola, New York: Dover Publications, Inc. 2009), 97

7. Gregory Berns, *Iconoclast* (Boston, Massachusetts: Harvard Business Press Corporation, 2008), 6

8. Ibid. 37

9. Ibid. 58

10. Gino Wickman, *Traction* (Dallas, Texas: BenBella Books, Inc., 2011), 29

11. Ibid. 30

12. Berns, *Iconoclast*, 130

13. Peter Senge, C. Otto Sharmer, Joseph Jaworski, Betty Sue Flowers, *Presence* (Cambridge, Massachusetts: The Society for Organizational Learning, Inc. 2004), 135

14. Margaret J. Wheatley, *Leadership and the New Science* (San Francisco, California: Barrett-Koehler Publishers, Inc., 1992), 53-54

15. Tim Brown, *Change By Design* (New York: HarperCollins Publishers, 2009), 3

16. Ibid. 7

17. Tom Kelley, *The Ten Faces Of Innovation* (New York: DoubleDay, 2005)

18. Modeste Tchaikovsky, *The Life and Letters of Peter Ilich Tchaikovsky* (New York, John Lane Company, 1906), 280-281

Chapter 6: Intelligence

1. Ken Robinson, "Do Schools Kill Creativity?" *TED Video*, filmed February 2006, https://www.ted.com/talks/ken_robinson_says_schools_kill_creativity?language=en

2. Elizabeth Landau, "The Brain's Amazing Potential for Recovery," *CNN/Health*, May 5, 2011, http://www.cnn.com/2011/HEALTH/05/05/brain.plasticity.giffords/#

3. Chade-Meng Tan, *Search Inside Yourself* (New York: HarperCollins, 2012), 3

4. Sue McGreevey, "Eight Weeks to a Better Brain," *Harvard Gazette*, (January 21, 2011): http://news.harvard.edu/gazette/story/2011/01/eight-weeks-to-a-better-brain/.

5. Ibid.

6. Daniel Goleman, "The Focused Leader," *Harvard Business Review*, December 2013, https://hbr.org/2013/12/the-focused-leader.

7. Rosen, *Grounded*.

8. Katie Davis, Joanna Christodoulou, Scott Seider, Howard Gardner, *The Theory of Multiple Intelligences*, http://multipleintelligencesoasis.org/wp-content/uploads/2013/06/443-davis-christodoulou-seider-mi-article.pdf

9. Daniel Goleman, *Working with Emotional Intelligence* (New York: Bantam Books, 1998)
10. Cindy Wigglesworth, SQ21: *The Twenty-One Skills of Spiritual Intelligence* (New York: Select Books, Inc., 2012), 8
11. Biomimicry Institute website, accessed January 2018, https://biomimicry.org/what-is-biomimicry/
12. Daniel H. Pink, *A Whole New Mind: Moving from the Information Age to the Conceptual Age* (New York: Penguin Group, 2005), 136-137
13. Howard Gardner, *Five Minds for the Future* (Boston: Harvard Business School Press, 2006), 2
14. Ibid. 3

Chapter 7: Initiative

1. Roberto Assagioli, *The Act of Will* (New York: Penguin Books, 1983), 10
2. Greg McKeown, *Essentialism: The Disciplined Pursuit of Less* (New York: Crown Publishing, 2014), 35-39
3. Viktor Frankl, *Man's Search for Meaning*, https://www.goodreads.com/author/quotes/2782.Viktor_E_Frankl
4. Roy F. Baumeister and John Tierney, *Willpower* (New York: Penguin Books, 2012) 28
5. Michael O'Brien, *Shift* (Palo Alto, California, Red Hill Publishing, 2017) 143
6. Bill George, *Authentic Leadership* (San Francisco, California: Jossey-Bass, 2003) 24-25
7. Jim Collins, *Good To Great* (New York: HarperCollins Publishers, 2001), 27, 30
8. Senge, Sharmer, Jaworski, and Flowers, *Presence*, 226

Chapter 8: Influence

1. Max DePree, *Leadership Is An Art* (New York: Bantam Doubleday Dell Publishing Group, 1989), 11
2. Ibid. 11
3. McKeown, *Essentialism: The Disciplined Pursuit of Less*, 60
4. Robert Bolton, *People Skills: How to Assert Yourself, Listen to Others, And Resolve Conflicts* (New York: Simon & Schuster, Inc., 1979)
5. From Ridge Associates bookmark that credits philosopher-theologian Martin Buber who advocated living life "on the narrow ridge."
6. Susan Scott, *Fierce Conversations* (New York: Viking Penguin, 2002), xiv
7. Granville Toogood, *The Articulate Executive* (New York, McGraw-Hill Companies, 1996), 49
8. Ibid. 15

9. Bradley P. Owens, Michael D. Johnson, Terrance R. Mitchell, "Expressed Humility in Organizations: Implications for Performance, Teams, and Leadership," *Organizational Science*, February 12, 2013, http://pubsonline.informs.org/doi/abs/10.1287/orsc.1120.0795

10. Andy Roberts, "Homer's Mentor: Duties Fulfilled or Misconstrued," *History of Education Journal*, (November 1999), http://citeseerx.ist.psu.edu/viewdoc/download;jsessionid=A202C5BBF1B12A710AF1210AAE76246E?doi=10.1.1.620.9451&rep=rep1&type=pdf

11. Tom Verducci, *The Cubs Way* (New York, Crown Archetype, 2017), 99

12. Aaron Churchill, Brian Barney, Alexa Hazel, Debra Kelsall, Sandy Mouch, Dominique Verdun, "What Is Stewardship and Should All Leaders Practice It," *New York Times InEducation*, 2015,http://nytimesineducation.com/spotlight/what-is-stewardship-and-should-all-great-leaders-practice-it/

Chapter 9: OUTcomes
1. Jim Collins, *Good To Great* (New York: HarperCollins Publishers, 2001), 21

PHOTO CREDITS

1	Boat © Dbajurin/Dreamstime.com
4	Exterior deck prism *Charles W. Morgan*, Mystic, CT
4	Deck prism *Schooner Adventuress*, Puget Sound, WA
15	Tree at Grand Canyon © Efaah0/Dreamstime.com
39	Elephants © Ronszoey/Dreamstime.com
65	Ice Crystals on Glass © David M. Kolb
87	Starry Sky © Rastan/Dreamstime.com
127	Owl © Photoquest/Dreamstime.com
163	Climb © Galyna Andrushko/Dreamstime.com
195	School of Fish © Dejan Sarman/Dreamstime.com
227	Water Drop © Katy Foster/Dreamstime.com
Cover	Author Photo © Tom Levin Photography

www.ingramcontent.com/pod-product-compliance
Lightning Source LLC
Chambersburg PA
CBHW021033210326
41598CB00016B/1002